STAINED GLASS WINDOWS:
THE LIFE AND DEATH OF JIMMY ZAPPALORTI

ROBERT ZAPPALORTI

The incidents depicted in this book are true or based on true events. Some names and events have been altered to preserve the narrative and/or people's privacy.

Words Take Flight Books printing: 2014

ISBN 13: 978-0692291771
ISBN 10: 0692291776

Printed in the United States of America

This book is dedicated to the memories of Mary T. Zappalorti,
Michael A. Zappalorti and James P. Zappalorti.
They are still loved and sorely missed.

In order to accurately recall and document events that happened within the family so long ago, I depended upon the combined memories of my older brother, Michael A. Zappalorti Jr. and my sister, Margaret M. Zappalorti-Marlow. Without their encouragement, guidance, help, and input this book could not have been written.

I wish to acknowledge the research talent and organizational skill of my friend, Jocelyn Little, who helped with the historic research on homosexuality, the history of New York City and the Gay Community of which portions were added to the text. Additionally, I extend my appreciation to my cousin, Elaine Zappalorti-Paralusz, who helped edited an early draft of the story. I'd also like to extend my gratitude to my four children, Debbie Zappalorti-Mournet, Kelly Zappalorti-Donahue, Robert Zappalorti Jr., and Michael J. Zappalorti III, who helped recall many of the happy and sad incidents put forth in this book. My children all loved their grandparents and their "Uncle Jimmy."

I would be remiss if I did not thank five individuals from the New York City Gay Community who were particularly helpful to the entire Zappalorti family (and me), right after Jimmy's murder, and for weeks, months and years afterwards. They are: Matt Forman, Patrick J. Suraci, James Smith, Bruce Kogan, and Robert ABert" Coffman. Bert founded The Zappalorti Society, which is a non-profit active support group for lesbian, gay, bisexual and/or transgendered people who also suffer from mental illness. I am also grateful to my friends, Professor Edward EmanuEL and Professor George Diestel for their suggestions, recommendations and additions to this story. I particularly want to thank Brent Monahan for proofreading and editing the entire manuscript and offered important comments which enhanced this book. Everyone mentioned above provided their wisdom and input to Jimmy's story which made the book's content much richer. Finally, this book is also dedicated to the families and victims of every hate crime, which is a sacrilege upon their memory.

Why I Wrote This Book

I DIDN'T SEE it coming; life broadsided me with many unforeseen tragedies. The sudden loss of a loved one or family member, for whatever reason, has a profound effect upon those people closest who are left behind. My brother, Jimmy Zappalorti, was murdered January 22, 1990, on the banks of the Arthur Kill River in Staten Island, New York. Even today, when I visit the site of his death I can still hear his anguished cries. No one came to help my brother on that tragic night so long ago, but many people from all walks of life rushed forward after his death. While the motive for Jimmy's murder was not the first in New York City based upon hate, it was the first that caused a firestorm of overwhelming concern and outrage by a community that could no longer be ignored by caring citizens and politicians of New York State. Such a warm outpouring of support meant a great deal to the entire Zappalorti family.

My brother's story starts the day of his birth in Brooklyn, New York; and touches upon his childhood there. The Zappalorti family moved to Charleston, Staten Island in 1950, where Jimmy attended Catholic grammar school and public high school. At age 17, he left Tottenville High School to join the US Navy, where he served on a combat ship during the Vietnam war. Jimmy met a gay man aboard ship who helped him accept the fact that he was homosexual. In Vietnam, he and his buddy were victims of a hate crime which caused him to suffer a nervous breakdown. When Jimmy returned home after being Honorably Discharged from the Navy, he was a changed man. He worked in the family stained glass business with his father and two older brothers, where he learned the specialized glass trade.

Jimmy also longed to play the piano and entertain people in bars and night clubs in New York City. On weekends he fled to Greenwich Village where he could find friendly people and warm acceptance. When traveling home at night from Manhattan, Jimmy was often the victim of robbery and beatings from muggers on the streets of New York, in subway stations, and at the Staten Island Ferry terminal. Aside from playing piano, Jimmy also liked gardening and landscaping. In order to earn extra money, he would cut lawns and hedges in town, so he could travel to faraway places. With the extra cash from his landscaping work and money he earned in the family glass business, Jimmy occasionally traveled around the United States and to Europe.

Being a homosexual, Jimmy struggled with his Catholic religious beliefs. He was also haunted by the memory of a beating he and his friend suffered in the Navy. To that end, he sought relief by sometimes drinking too much. During the summer he would sit on the beach of the Arthur Kill River and watch sunsets while sipping beer. On one of those nights he decided to build himself a shack on the river. A place of his own that would be his sanctuary. To build his beach house, he collected drift wood from the river and old windows from the family glass business. Over time his shack took shape with a large kitchen and kerosene stove for heat. The bedroom had a big picture window that faced the river, so when he lay in bed he could see boats passing and the silhouette of the Outerbridge Crossing.

In 1989, two young men moved into Charleston who disliked Jimmy because he was gay. These men insulted, harassed and tormented him. When Jimmy showed no fear and stood-up to them, they decided to get even. One night in January of 1990, these two men attacked Jimmy in his shack, stabbed him, slit his throat and threw him in the river. Details of the police investigation and the subsequent arrest of these men are chronicled. Jimmy's story continues after his death during the immediate aftermath due to strong interest by citizens groups, politicians and gay activist organizations, who pushed for the passing of a hate crime bill in Albany, New York.

Jimmy's story ends with me digging three holes to plant trees in my brother's memory. On the day I planted those trees the life-long condition of coping with traumatic loss began for me and continues to today. Each and every one of us copes with traumatic loss in our own way. I have chosen to cope with this tragedy by sharing the story of Jimmy and my family with gratitude. Gratitude is powerful. It enlightens the days of sorrow and grief with positivity. I'm grateful to so many people who helped me and my family cope with grief. They are part of my support group, and I am part of theirs.

In particular, my brother Mike, my sister Peggy, and I all went through a prolonged period of mourning as survivors, but my particular way of coping was writing. In order to create this book, I had to research various events that happened to Jimmy when he was away from the family in New York City, especially while traveling abroad. I also depended upon various newspaper stories and reports about Jimmy's murder and his murderers. I researched the fine police work of the two detectives who investigated the case, with my parents when they were still alive, with my older brother and sister, and with my parish priest. By remembering my loving parents and my brother Jimmy, and what my older brother and sister, Mike and Peggy, went through as survivors, writing this book helped me stay connected with my family and with whom I am.

I wrote this book to thank those who helped me and my family through an unexpected ordeal. I also wrote it to perhaps help other survivors or families, professionals, community volunteers, police, journalists, ministers, priests and in my case, many New York public officials. This is narrative nonfiction, family saga; it's a true crime story about my younger brother and my New York City community. Jimmy's story may remind you of someone you knew or have known. History and our religious traditions are full of cases of those who persevered despite the continuing trauma from the loss of a loved one. My story also includes the fact that a major public law in the state of New York had my brother's name associated with it during the bill signing ceremony. A hate crimes bill was enacted and signed into law by Governor George Pataki in the year 2000. Few family losses from a hate crime bear such a positive and public outcome.

I'm a herpetologist and wildlife consultant by profession; herpetology is the study of amphibians and reptiles, which includes snakes. I know that many people fear, misunderstand and some may even hate snakes, similar to the way that some people dislike or hate human behavior which is different from what they consider the norm. Rather than being too judgmental, we should all endeavor to be more tolerant of other behaviors, to live and let live. Hate and intolerance is what killed my brother, Jimmy.

Today, many people's attitudes are changing for the better. In recent years, an increasing number of our citizens have now opened their hearts and are more tolerant and understanding of those who had been perceived as different. To those people I offer a special thank you. However, before reading this book, you should know that certain persons, some characters names, or place names have been changed or fictionalized for privacy purposes. Nevertheless, I endeavored to tell Jimmy's story with as much factual detail as I could research and remember.

Chapter 1 - Learning of Jimmy's Death

WHEN SOMETHING SHOCKING happens that impacts your life, you can remember where you were when you learn of bad news or tragedy. For example, when John F. Kennedy was assassinated by Lee Harvey Oswald on Friday, November 22, 1963, in Dallas, Texas, when Martin Luther King was assassinated by James Earl Ray in Memphis, Tennessee on April 4, 1968, or when terrorists flew two jet airliners into the Twin Towers in lower Manhattan on September 11, 2001. To the rest of the people in New York, or throughout the country, Jimmy's murder was insignificant compared with the abovementioned historical events. But to the Zappalorti family, Jimmy's murder was every bit as shocking and traumatic.

When I learned of Jimmy's murder I was at Resorts Casino in Atlantic City with my ex-wife, Peggy Vargas. We were there for a slot tournament and to see a comedy show. What I remember mostly about it was the paranormal dream I had that night. A strange dream, that continues to haunt me to this day. I share my dream from notes I took directly after the night of January 22, 1990.

In my dream, the night was choked with fog, and the streets were empty except for a skinny, ten-year-old boy. Young Jimmy Zappalorti ran wildly down the dark street, being chased by two thugs in leather jackets. Jimmy wore blue jeans and white mud-streaked tee-shirt. He dashed around a corner and nearly collided with his brother, Robert. Jimmy recognized him and hugged him. Robert hugged him back, but noticed that his clothes were all wet. Jimmy's face was contorted with terror.

"Bobby! Help! They're after me."

"Who's after you? Why are you all wet?"

"Two guys threw me in the river," Jimmy said. "I'm cold Bobby, I'm very cold! They're trying to hurt me."

Robert took a quick look around the corner. The two bullies approached. They were stocky, well-built and tall. They wore leather jackets. One had a knife in his hand. Robert could not make out their faces, other than to see that one had scruffy hair.

They were searching in doorways and behind parked cars, and they were getting closer.

"Let's get out of here," the dream Robert said anxiously.

Jimmy and Robert hurried along the dark street but heard the voices of the thugs close behind them.

"There he is!" one of the thugs yelled, "I see the little sissy!"

The other thug shouted, "We're gonna get you, so stop running!"

Jimmy was falling behind and could not keep up because his short legs were starting to tire. Robert picked Jimmy up and carried him. They ran through an alley, past some parked cars, weather-beaten buildings, and small houses. An abandoned storefront was in front of them, so they opened the unlocked door and ran inside to hide. An old curtain lay on the floor; Robert put it in front of the window, so the thugs could not see inside. Robert held his little brother protectively as he peeked from behind the curtain.

In the moonlight he could see both thugs in the street and could hear them talking. They argued over which way to go. Eventually they ran back up the street. After a short time Robert grabbed Jimmy's hand and they ran out of the store, down the street, and across an open grassy field towards the Arthur Kill River.

They came to a sand path that was lined with massive stands of giant reed, red maple and swamp willow. Fog rose from the marsh as they ran across an open, moonlit sandbar toward a shack on the edge of the river. Lights of the New Jersey shoreline glowed across the river and the lit silhouette of the Outerbridge was in the background. Somehow, the two thugs had doubled back and saw Jimmy and Robert as they crossed the sandbar. The chase was on again. Robert and Jimmy reached the cabin, opened the door and dashed inside the dark room. Robert bolted the sturdy wooden door behind them. Inside the simple, two-room, wood frame cabin was a table, chairs, and a kerosene burning stove in the kitchen. The second room had a bed, a bookcase, an end table, and an armchair. Moonlight shone through the large picture window in the bedroom that had clear stained glass panels on both sides, which overlooked the river. Robert walked Jimmy into the bedroom. "Jimmy, hide under the bed," Robert commanded.

"Okay, but I'm scared."

Jimmy crawled under the bed and hid in the shadows. From his point-of-view, he looked at a patch of moonlight coming through a stained glass window as it lit the wooden floor. Robert went back into the front room and looked around for a weapon. He saw a baseball bat in the corner, grabbed it, then stood behind the door and listened. He could hear the voices of the thugs as they approached the cabin. The thugs tried to open the door, but it was locked.

"We know you assholes are in there!" one of them yelled.

"Open the door or we'll kick it down!" shouted the other.

They began to push and pound the door. One growled, "Come on, and help me push it in."

Both forcefully put their shoulders to the door. The hinges and bolt began to weaken.

Robert shouted, "What do you want with my brother? Leave us alone!"

A voice yelled from behind the door, "We'll kick this door down, kick your ass, and get your brother anyway!"

"I have a bat," Robert threatened. "I'll use it if you come in."

A thug said angrily, "Your bat don't scare us!"

The attackers pushed and pounded on the door even harder,

causing the hinges to suddenly pull away from the molding. The wooden door crashed inward and landed on top of Robert, forcing him to the floor on his back. One of the thugs quickly grabbed the bat from Robert's hand and whacked him across the forehead. The force of the blow cut his head and dazed him. The other thug searched around the cabin for Jimmy. He went into the bedroom, where he saw the tip of Jimmy's foot sticking-out from under the bed. He beckoned to his buddy who came in. From Jimmy's point-of-view, he saw their feet approaching the bed. Jimmy whispered fearfully to himself, "Bobby, help!"

However, Robert could not help him because he lay on the floor bleeding and unconscious.

The bearded thug reached under and grabbed Jimmy's leg. Jimmy screamed and kicked at his hands with his other foot.

The thug growled, "Grab his hands and hold him. Stop squirming, you little shit, or I'll break your leg."

Jimmy kicked and screamed even more, "Let me go, leave me alone! Bobby!"

The two thugs dragged little Jimmy out from under the bed. One was holding his arms and the other had his legs. Jimmy looked in the other room and saw his big brother lying on the floor moaning and bleeding. His brother, Bobby could not help. No one could help him. The two thugs looked at the large picture window with stained glass panels and smiled at each other. They began to swing Jimmy back and forth. One said, "On three; we throw his ass through the window."

"Okay: one, two, three!"

They released their hold and forcefully flung Jimmy at the window. He crashed through and plunged from view into the darkness, yelling. The two thugs laughed as Jimmy screamed in pain. The sound of shattering glass echoed in the foggy night!"

The sound of breaking glass merged with and became the sound of a telephone ringing in my hotel room at Resorts Casino. I aroused out of a deep sleep to answer the phone.

"Hello?"

A telephone operator said, "Your 8:00 AM wake-up call, Mr. Zappalorti."

"Oh, okay, operator. Thank you."

I lay there for a moment remembering the troubling dream from which I had just awoken. I turned and shook my girlfriend, Peggy Vargas who was lying next to me. She noticed the worried expression on my face.

"What's wrong Rob?"

"I had this terrible dream about Jimmy." I told her about my dream. Peggy leaned over, gave me a kiss on the cheek and got out of bed. She looked stunning as she walked towards the bathroom wearing a black silk nightgown.

"It was just a dream. Come take a shower with me. I'll help you forget it," Peggy said. I slowly stood up and followed her into the bathroom. She was right; I did not give the strange dream another thought.

Later that day, Peggy and I were in the casino, where numerous hopeful gamblers were feeding coins into the slot machines. The slot tournament was in progress within a roped-off section of the casino. Others gamblers were busy at blackjack, roulette, and craps tables, while dealers collected chips. The air was filled with the smell of cigarette and cigar smoke while the sound of ringing bells, chimes, and shouted conversations merged in a din.

Peggy was at a slot machine, looking disappointed. The woman next to her was all smiles as she hit triple bars. Peggy looked at me, as I watched from the sideline.

"Darn!" Peggy said. "I never have any luck."

A woman announcer spoke via the public address system: "Mr. Robert Zappalorti, please pick up a house phone."

Marveling at being paged in the casino, I found a house phone and identified myself to the operator. My oldest son came on the line. In a tight, quavering voice, Bobby related that Uncle Jimmy had been murdered the previous night.

After asking a few questions that could not yet be answered, I said, "Okay, I'll leave here as soon as I can and drive up to Staten Island. Will you be at your grandparents' house?"

Robert Jr. answered, "Yeah, I'm here now. And dad, I'm sorry about Uncle Jimmy."

I hung up the telephone and walked through the crowded casino in a daze. I began to weep and wiped tears that were trickling down my cheeks. I walked towards the craps table where Peggy was gambling and delivered the news.

While Peggy packed, I called my parents house on Staten Island.

"Bobby," my father began in a voice broken with emotion, "We've been trying to get in touch with you all day. They killed my son! They killed my poor Jimmy."

The drive to Staten Island would take almost three hours. I tried to concentrate well enough to drive safely. I gazed at the highway without speaking, engrossed in deep thought. Then the strange dream from night before snapped sharply into my consciousness.

"Peggy, my dream last night! I told you about the two guys chasing Jimmy."

"That's right! You did say something about a bad dream. How odd. Could you have had a premonition?"

"I'm not sure what it was. All I know is that it made no sense to me this morning when I woke. But, now it does. Now I know why! My brother was calling out for help, but no one was there to help him. No one, but his murderer."

As the car hurled northward on the Garden State Parkway, I stared at the road ahead through the windshield in silence. I vibrated with anger, feeling impotent at not having been there to help my brother, Jimmy. I felt rage mixed with a profound regret that he would never see my younger brother alive again.

I now invite you to come along with me on this mental journey back in time. Read the highlights of Jimmy's life and times from when he was born on September 29, 1945, in the Bay Ridge section of Brooklyn, until his death on January 23, 1990, on Staten Island, New York. I also include the aftermath which illustrates many of the good people who came forward to help the Zappalorti family, and all the wonderful things they did and have done to honor Jimmy's memory.

Chapter 2 - Welcome to the Zappalorti Family

A PANE OF glass cannot remain in place without a frame. Similarly, to undertsand the life – and death – of Jimmy Zappalorti, you need to understand what "framed" who he was and, in many ways, still is: family.

Mary Theresa Zappalorti stood at her kitchen stove, cooking breakfast for her husband and three young children. She had sky-blue eyes and long, brown hair that flowed down over her shoulders. Mary was an attractive thirty-year old Irish woman. She wore a yellow-and-green flowered print dress and a matching green apron and was nine months pregnant with her fourth child. She was a kind, soft-spoken, attractive, energetic and devoted wife and mother to her growing family.

Michael Angelo Zappalorti Sr. was a tall, handsome man with dark brown hair and eyes that strongly revealed his Latino and Italian heritage. Mike was a serious-looking man with a neatly-trimmed, narrow mustache; his parted hair was slicked back. He was dressed in blue overalls, a blue shirt, and work boots. He was sitting at the kitchen table with Michael Jr., the oldest son (whom the family called Mickey) and his little brother, Robert, called Bobby. The household was rounded out by Margaret, affectionately known as Peggy. Dad was 32, Mickey 9, Bobby 4 and Peggy 7.

It was a typical day in the Zappalorti household. The phone rang –

it was a customer with a big job. Mike worked hard to provide for his family, all with an eye on moving them out of Brooklyn. The house was getting small for the growing family: three children shared a bedroom, while a Castro convertible couch served as the parents' bed.

Everyone worked. Young Peggy helped her Mom with the cooking and cared for her younger brother, Bobby, after school hours, while Mary tended to customers in the stained glass window store. Mike often looked at his wife, concerned about her impending pregnancy. She would laugh and say how can I stay off of my feet when I have to take care of three kids and help you run your business?

The kitchen was the heart of the home on 7415 Third Avenue, Brooklyn, which served as the same address for the Zappalorti glass studio and store. Up the hallway from the kitchen was a curtain that separated the modest living quarters from the storefront. In the workshop, a very large worktable on wooden horses took up most of the space. Assorted diamond-tipped glass cutters, T-squares, straight-edge rulers and other tools were gathered at one end of the worktable. A half-completed stained glass window lay flat on the rest of the table. Storage racks with a rainbow array of colored glass panels lined the walls. A narrow hallway connected the next room, the store and public reception area. Displays of various picture frames and mirror samples were neatly arranged. A glass counter held fancy mirrors, sample frames and assorted blown-glass animals for sale.

The display window was illuminated with colorful stained glass window panels and glass figures. Behind the counter were framed displays of brightly colored, mounted butterflies. Another panel contained an extensive stamp collection from all over the world. Both collections were Mike's long-time hobbies. Clearly, the store was a showplace for both a talented glass artist, and an avid stamp and butterfly collector.

At the curb was parked a Ford panel truck, with lettering on both sides that read, "Michael's Glass Company, Stained and Leaded Glass Windows." There was a wooden rack on the roof for hauling ladders and another rack inside the panel truck on the passenger's side for transporting sheets of clear window glass and stained glass windows.

Mike opened his own stained glass studio in Brooklyn after his father, Hector, died in 1942. Ettore "Hector" Zappalorti was born in Genoa, a seaport in northeastern Italy, where he learned the art of stained glassmaking from his father. Ettore first immigrated to Buenos Aires, Argentina, more than 7,500 sea miles away from his birthplace. He had four sons with his wife, Sophie, who was born in Buenos Aires: Ettore Jr., Dante, Enrique and Miguel Angelo. The spoken language in their household was Spanish. Their eldest son, Ettore Jr., never went to America, remaining in Buenos Aires with his wife and two children. The rest of the family immigrated to New York in 1922.

Like so many other immigrants, the Zappalortis passed through Ellis Island. Miguel Angelo, the youngest, was ten years old. His name was anglicized to Michael, but his first language was Spanish, along with some Italian that he learned from his father. Ettore became Hector and Enrique became Henry. In 1924, Hector Zappalorti opened the first Zappalorti-owned stained glass studio in Hell's Kitchen, a notoriously tough neighborhood on the Lower West Side waterfront of Manhattan. Young Michael helped his father in the glass studio, did chores for his mother and made friends with some Italian and Polish boys who lived on his block. He joined the Boy Scouts, eventually becoming an Eagle Scout.

Mike fashioned himself after Rudolf Valentino – but his dashing looks and dressing hid a ferocious temper. He channeled this anger into his training as a middleweight Golden Gloves boxer, dropping out of the sport only at the insistence of his father and mother.

At 19 years old, Mike got into a fight with three neighborhood street toughs from a gang called the Westies after they called him a "spic." Thanks to his boxing experience, Mike was holding his own until all three grabbed him and threw him through a glass storefront window. The three Westies ran away and left Mike lying in a pool of blood, his right leg broken and and so severely cut by the shattered glass that it required 50 stitches to repair. The damage was far reaching: during World War II, Mike was classified as 4-F and unable to serve. Instead, he went to work for the Civilian Conservation Corps and later for the Work Program of America.

In the summer of 1933, when he was 21, Mike met Mary Ryan, also of Brooklyn, through a mutual friend. Like Mike, Mary's family had immigrated to America – only the Ryan's had begun their journey in County Cork, Ireland, in 1910. Mary came from a large family: a twin sister, Nora; three older brothers – Tom, Eddie and Jack; a younger brother, Martin; and a younger sister, Regina. After a one-year courtship and winning over her older brothers, who mistrusted this "ladies man," Mike and Mary were married in 1934, beginning their 61-year life together.

When Hector Zappalorti died in February 1942, his three sons all started their own stained glass window businesses. Mike's oldest brother, Dante, opened his glass business in Englewood, New Jersey. Henry and Mike both stayed in Brooklyn and started their businesses on Third Avenue, one mile apart : Henry's on the corner of Third and 69th Street, while Mike's store was on Third between 74th and 75th Streets.

Late September 1945. World War II had just ended. Servicemen from all branches of the military were coming home to pick up their lives. There was a feeling of optimism and relief in the air, a desire for home and family – and in the Zappalorti household, the family was about to get bigger.

One day not long after Mike had begun a stained glass project at

Brooklyn's Saint John The Baptist Roman Catholic Church, Mary was busy minding the store and doing household chores. While carrying a loaded laundry basked, a sharp pain in her lower abdomen made her wince and dropped her to her knees. Terrified, she reached under her dress and withdrew a blood-soaked hand. Oh my God. I'm having a miscarriage.

Mary yelled out for her four-year-old son Bobby and struggled to a wooden folding chair at the table. Bobby's eyes widened and his face whitened as he saw the blood on her hands and dress. "Mommy! What's wrong? Why are you bleeding?" Mary replied consolingly, trying conceal her alarm, "I pinched my leg on the wooden chair and cut myself, Mary lied," she lied. "Run next door and get Bertha. Tell her to come right away. Go now!"

Bobby burst into the dry cleaning store. Bertha was a kindly, heavy-set woman of about forty with brown hair going to gray. She sat behind the counter, sorting shirts when Bobby startled her, shouting, "Mrs. Anderson, come right away! Mommy cut her leg!"

When Bertha and Bobby reached the Zappalorti kitchen, Mary was sitting at the table. She told Bobby as calmly as she could to go play. Then she related to Bertha her fears of a miscarriage.

Hours later, Mary Zappalorti was in a bed in the recovery room at Kings County Hospital. A nurse in a starched white uniform and white cap checked her pulse and temperature. Another nurse entered carrying a baby wrapped in a blue blanket. The nurse glowed. "Mrs. Zappalorti, I have someone for you to meet!" She held out the newborn baby: eight pounds, five ounces and perfectly healthy.

Tired and happy, Mary took the baby in her arms. Smiling into his face she said, "Your name will be James Patrick, after Saint James and Saint Patrick of Ireland."

18

Chapter 3 - Family Life in Brooklyn

THE NEW BABY, James Patrick Zappalorti, was the center of the family. While her mother was busy tending to customers in the store, Peggy helped by babysitting little Jimmy after school and on weekends. Being the baby in the family, Jimmy was popular with all the relatives. Mike, Mary and his siblings bathed Jimmy in attention and affection. Grandfather Tom Ryan nicknamed him "Jiminy Cricket."

These were good times.

The back kitchen of the Zappalorti business and home was a gathering place for friends and family. On weekends, Mike and Mary entertained in their small quarters, especially playing cards with relatives and friends. Poker was the game of choice whenever Bertha and her husband, John, visited, or Mary's three brothers and their wives would come over. Mary's brother, Martin "Buster" Ryan and his new wife, Esther, became very close with Mike and Mary.

In the summer of 1948, a three bedroom apartment became available on the top floor of the building at 7415 Third Avenue. Mike and Mary needed more room, while Mike needed more space for his glass store. Uncle Buster, Aunt Esther and their new baby, Martin Jr., also needed a larger apartment, so both families decided to pool their resources by sharing the apartment and splitting the cost of the rent. The Ryans took the back two rooms, which included the kitchen and only bathroom – and so was created a logistical nightmare.

Around this time, Mike's stained glass business was doing so well that he purchased a 1940 black Ford panel truck. He also hired another assistant, Harry Doll, as an addition to his existing assistant, Roy Canal. Together, they worked in churches all over the metropolitan area. Then in the spring of 1949, Mike ordered a large new storefront sign which read: "Michael's Glass Studio – Stained and Leaded Glass, Residential Windows, Mirrors, Table Tops and Picture Frames."

Like Mickey and Bobby, little Jimmy watched his father work in the glass studio and helped him as soon as he was old enough. Mike gave him a toy toolbox, which Jimmy proudly carried about. Jimmy was a shy little boy who adored his family and always wanted to be a part of the action.

One day in the summer of 1949, when Jimmy was four-and-a-half years old, Mike and Roy were loading sections of stained glass windows onto the glass rack of the panel truck. Jimmy stood on the sidewalk holding his tool box, watching with a child's open-mouthed fascination as they carefully placed the windows on the glass wrack. After the men had finished tying down the work, Jimmy pleaded with his father to go with him. Mike demurred saying that Jimmy was too young and that he should stay home with his mother. This didn't sit well with the young "apprentice."

Instead of going back into the store, and with tool box in hand, Jimmy opened the back door and climbed into the panel truck. With the radio playing, the two men talking, and a stack of boxes and tools stacked behind them, Mike and Roy did not see or hear the door open. Jimmy pulled the door closed, but it did not lock, and then hid by covering himself with a folded blanket in the back of the truck.

Fortunately, from inside the glass store, Mary and Peggy were looking out the front window. Mary had seen Jimmy clambering into the back of the truck. Mary gasped and ran out the front door in an instant with Peggy running behind. Mary shouted just as Mike began to pull away from the curb.

Roy saw Mary running toward the truck and told Mike, who stopped and backed up to the curb. He got out and walked toward his wife. When he asked why she stopped him, she opened the back door and pointed at the moving blanket. When Mike picked it up, Jimmy's head popped out. The boy stared at his father with tears in his eyes. "I just wanted to help you, Daddy!" he cried. Roy turned to Mike and said with a grin, "He's just like you — he's stubborn and won't take 'no' for an answer."

Jimmy's fascination with his father's work in stained glass continued to grow as he did. Because the children lived where Mike conducted business and made the windows, it was common for them to be in the glass shop. However, he always warned them of the danger of glass and how easy it was to get cut. Mike would always tell his children, "You have to learn to respect glass and always use caution, but don't be afraid to handle it."

The following year in the spring of 1950, Jimmy was now in kindergarten classes at Our Lady of Angels Catholic School, where the rest of the Zappalorti children had attended. Jimmy was a little taller and thinner than an average five-year-old. Both he and older brother Bobby liked watching their father make stained glass windows in the shop, but Jimmy's legs were too short to see what was going on at the top of the workbench from the floor. Because Bobby was five years older and taller, he could easily climb up on the cross brace of the wooden horses that supported the workbenches and watch his father work. Jimmy struggled, but with great effort he managed to climb up. Once up there, he would fold his arms and place his elbows on the top of the bench, giving him balance and a good view of what his father was doing. Jimmy would sometimes play with the colorful pieces of scrap glass while his father worked. He would often say, "My Daddy is putting a puzzle together."

One early afternoon, Roy and Mike were busy cutting colored

glass for a synagogue in Bensonhurst, Brooklyn. Mary came into the shop from behind the kitchen curtain. She asked about progress on the new windows, then left to do errands. When she returned, she had Jimmy in tow.

Holding up a piece of paper, Jimmy said, "Look Dad! I got a gold star on my spelling test." Mike took the paper in his hand and said, "Very good – that's my boy! You have to learn to read and write, so you can run my business someday." Jimmy proudly replied, "When I get big I'll make pretty windows, just like you!"

Jimmy climbed up the wooden horse under the bench as he always did. He asked, "What are you working on, Dad?" From the other side of the workbench, Mike looked at Jimmy and said, "The Star of David, son." As the words were spoken, Jimmy's feet slipped from the wooden brace on the horse. He instantly fell backwards, landing on a pane of red glass that Roy had placed against the wall earlier. From where Mike stood, he could not see his littlest son – all he could only hear was the shattering of glass...then silence.

Mike dashed around the bench at exactly the same time Mary came running from the kitchen, where the sound of broken glass had carried. They both looked down at Jimmy, who lay perfectly still on the floor, surrounded by thousands of shards of broken red glass. Jimmy looked up at his parents and started to cry. Mike scooped his son up off the floor frantically asking, "Are you alright?! did you get cut?!"

Mary, with equal nervous speed, searched Jimmy's head, neck, arms and legs: no cuts, no blood, not a scratch. There were no cuts, no blood, not a scratch on him. Mike reassured Jimmy, hugged him and said, "It's okay, don't cry. It was just an accident. You're not hurt." The adults stood there in disbelief that Jimmy was not seriously cut after landing on the sheet of glass. As Mary took Jimmy from Mike, she said, "It's a miracle he wasn't cut. God was watching over him."

Mike sighed with relief and said, "When I first looked down at him on the floor, I thought the red glass was blood. This kid really must be blessed by God!"

24

Chapter 4 - Family Life on Staten Island

WITH EVER MORE people crowding into Brooklyn, Mike and Mary Zappalorti knew they needed to move to a larger and more suitable living quarters. In October of 1950, the family of six and their pet dog, Rex, moved to the town of Charleston in Richmond County – at the time, the official name for Staten Island.

The borough of Staten Island is the southernmost and most remote of New York City's five boroughs It had long been a good place for New Yorkers to escape from busy city life. Sometimes called "the forgotten borough," Staten Island may be best known as the dumping ground for the rest of the city's trash: the huge Fresh Kills Landfill is just north of Charleston. Other than car thefts and vandalism, the borough's crime rate was low and predominated by working- and lower-middle-class families.

Staten Island had even more churches and other houses of worship than Brooklyn did, which made it a great location for a stained glass business. The Zappalorti's found a two-story, three-bedroom house for sale on a quiet, dead-end street. At last, Mike and Mary had their own bedroom. Peggy had her own room, too. The three boys shared the third, large, upstairs bedroom. Mickey was fourteen, Peggy twelve, Bobby almost ten and Jimmy five years old when they moved from Brooklyn.

What had truly sold Mike on the Androvette Street property was a large yard with a separate garage. He saw that there was enough space to build his ideal stained glass studio and store. Soon after they moved in, Mike tore down the old wood-frame garage and built a roomy cement-block studio from the ground up. The left side of the building had cathedral ceilings and tall windows let in plenty of light and air. He built several work tables, big enough to work on more than one stained glass window at a time, and a number of shelves and colored glass storage bins. The store entrance was to the left of the building and the garage door was big enough to park the glass truck inside. At the end of the day, Mike could just close the garage door and take a few steps to go inside his own roomy house.

Owning his own home and studio meant no more paying rent to someone else and no more long drives to Brooklyn fighting the rush hour traffic. Friendly neighbors —like Charlie and Esther Kosa; their two daughters, Carol and Ester; and son, Charlie Jr. – helped make it a desirable place to live.

The family joined St. Joseph's Roman Catholic Church in Rossville, and both Mary and Mike were active members. Confident and proud of his workmanship, Mike convinced the parish monsignor that the church windows needed replacement. Once he had his artwork locally displayed, Mike found plenty of business replacing windows of other churches and of synagogues throughout Staten Island.

One day in July 1954, the three Zappalorti brothers – Mickey, Bobby and Jimmy —were home watching television while their father was at work. Jimmy started getting restless and kept asking, "When's Mom coming home from grocery shopping?" Tiring of Bobby and Mickey's answers of "Shh!" and "Soon," Jimmy decided to go play on the sandbar down by the river. Bobby's first thought was to ask Jimmy to bring back any frogs or toads he caught – he loved the wetlands and its animals, which led to his profession later in life. Mickey's concern was for Jimmy's safety and his own: "The tide's in, so don't go near the river. Mom told me to watch you!" Jimmy promised to stay on the sandbar and ran out the door.

Jimmy walked onto a large sandbar, in reality dredge-spoil from the Arthur Kill River. Thick patches of swamp reeds, switch grass and broom sedge formed a wall along both sides of the sand lot. A small pond half filled with water was directly in front of him. Cattails grew from the pond.

After some time trying to catch frogs, he noticed all of the twigs and branches lying around, and decided to build a campfire. Jimmy collected burning material into a pile and pulled out a pack of matches from his pocket. He struck a few, but couldn't get the fire started. Finally, he was able to ignite a clump of dried grass, kept cupped inside his hands, and the flames took off – and with disastrous results.

The campfire started to burn; but suddenly a rush of wind sent the fire into the dry brush around where Jimmy had intended to camp. Panicking, Jimmy tried to stomp out the flames; but the wind was too strong and soon the fire was out of control.

Jimmy burst through the front door and breathlessly told his brothers what he had done. Bobby and Mickey ran outside and down the street where, to their amazement, there was a wall of flames coming from the woods that could be seen over the six-foot-high fence edging Charlie Kosa's yard.

"I'd better call the fire department!" Mickey said. To which Bobby added, "Better call two!" All the while, Jimmy moaned, "Daddy's gonna kill me!"

Four firetrucks, one police car and many firemen later, and the blaze was out. After a brief consultation, the fire chief and police sergeant decided that the Zappalorti kids didn't intentionally set the fire. By now, Mary Zappalorti had arrived and began an inquisitor-style questioning of her sons. When she found out it was Jimmy who had been playing with fire, she yelled at him to go home, go to his room and await his father's return from work.

As she angrily watched him slink away, she thought how, again, the Lord had watched over her youngest son. But the thought, "For how much longer?" lingered.

Chapter 5 - I Just Want to Join the Navy

SOON, THE ZAPPALORTI children had grown into teenagers and were graduating, one by one, from Tottenville High School.

With one exception.

Mickey, the oldest child, graduated in June 1954. In June 1962, Mike Jr. met his future wife, Carol, at a mutual friend's house on Staten Island, and were were married the following May. Peggy took a job in Manhattan and, the following year, married Harry Coleman, from Rosebank, Staten Island. Bobby graduated in 1959, after which he and his good friend, Jim Anderson, started a failed do-wop group called The Dreams. They later started a five-piece band called The Careless Five. While playing with the band at a popular night club in Midland Beach, Staten Island, Bobby met Leticia Ruth Cummings. They fell in love and were married in September 1961.

Meanwhile, Jimmy was unhappy and wanted to escape from Tottenville High School and the small town of Charleston – and the Navy, he felt, was his way out. So, in October 1962, Jimmy and his parents were summoned for a conference with Sam Weening, the high school guidance counselor. The four of them sat in the counselor's office in uncomfortable silence while Mr. Weening looked over the records.

The counselor asked Jimmy why he wasn't applying himself and said with some foreboding that Jimmy would be a failure without a high school diploma. Mr. Weening also noted a number of fights into which Jimmy had gotten with older boys. All of this prompted Jimmy to turn to his father and tell him that he didn't like school, that he wasn't learning and that he was tired of both being picked on and going to school. "I just want to leave and join the Navy," he said.

Mary jumped in and echoed Jimmy's sentiments. She said that her son felt that he could learn more in the Navy, and that the recruiting officer had told them that Jimmy could get his high school equivalency diploma as part of his training. Weening tried to talk the senior and junior Zappalorti out of it, but ultimately agreed that the Navy might offer the boy a more disciplined environment.

Reluctantly, Jimmy's parents authorized his enlistment by signing the consent form. The following day, Jimmy went to the Navy recruitment office with his signed enlistment papers.

At seventeen, Jimmy was in the Navy.

Chapter 6 - Jimmy's Navy Years

JAMES PATRICK ZAPPALORTI was stationed at the U.S. Naval Training Center in Great Lakes, Illinois, where he completed basic training in 1963. After his graduation, he became a Seaman Apprentice, then a S.N. (Seaman) E-3. Jimmy was assigned to the USS Henrico, an attack transport ship commissioned in 1943, which had landed troops on Omaha Beach on D-Day. The USS Henrico was also part of the task group that landed the first U. S. combat unit in South Vietnam: at Da Nang, Hue and Chu Lai.

On February 2, 1965, at 0730 hours, a group of sailors were doing jumping jacks to the vocal cadence of their officer, Ensign Tom Johnson. Ensign Johnson ordered them to stop and announced that twenty-four hour shore leave was posted on the duty board. All hands up for shore leave would leave no later than 1700 hours.

Ensign Tom Johnson was a 26-year-old San Franciscan with sky-blue eyes and brown hair, and a rugged appearance and a muscular build from lifting weights. He had joined the Navy at age 19 in 1958 and had ultimately been promoted to ensign, the most junior commissioned officer. But had his commanding officers or fellow shipmates known the secret he harbored and only shared with extreme discretion, his career would have gone much differently: dishonorable discharge, a stint in a military prison or even in a mental ward.

Ensign Johnson was bisexual.

Hearing the words "shore leave" sent the men running for the duty board below decks. Jimmy ran after them. But he was halted by the ensign's call. What ensued was an informal interrogation, about Jimmy's home, his penchant for keeping to himself, that the letters he received were not from a sweetheart. Johnson dismissed the sailor, watched him jog off and then walked to his own quarters.

The Henrico was docked at Subic Bay Naval Base, in the Republic of the Philippines. The following afternoon, Jimmy and two buddies prepared to go dockside to explore Olangapo City, the major port near the base. Fred Brown and Joe O'Brian were both two years older than and Jimmy. They caught a cab to Main Street in Olangapo City, a thoroughfare filled with civilians, sailors and Marines. Clothing shops, food markets and restaurants were interspersed among the omnipresent bars. Music blared; call girls beckoned in front of the night clubs. Fred, Joey and Jimmy reveled in the sights and sounds.

Fred and Joey were intently eyeing the hookers and teased Jimmy asking him if he "wanted some." When Jimmy asked what they were talking about, the two men burst into laughter.

They entered a crowded, sleazy bar called The Bamboo Lounge. The place reeked of cigarette smoke, sour beer and fried fish. Sailors, marines and bar girls filled the tables. In one corner of the bar, a Filipino man played '50s rock on an out-of-tune piano. The place was pure cliché from front to back. While Fred and Joey made their way to the bar and ordered drinks, Jimmy wandered over to the piano. He stared intently at the piano player's hands as they flew up and down the keyboard. When the player asked Jimmy if he played, he nodded yes.

By then, Fred and Joey had returned with two bottles of whiskey and three busty call girls, one of whom took Jimmy's hand. Fred whispered in Jimmy's ear, "You ever been laid?" Jimmy lied, "Yeah. Plenty of times." The impatient call girl dragged Jimmy to a private room, as dingy as it was small.

Jimmy looked at the queen-sized bed sagging along one wall, covered dirty sheets and a pillow, while the girl lit a cigarette and a candle with the same match. She asked in a bored tone, "What do you want, sailor boy?" and started the negotiation process as to what and how much.

Jimmy tried to feign interest and comfort, but he had to be honest, telling her that he didn't want anything - and that there really wasn't anything she could do for him. The call girl was puzzled at first and pressed him. He told her she was very pretty, but that he was...

"Queer," she finished.

Jimmy quickly said, "No! I'm not queer. Why did you say that?" The woman replied that she knew what she was talking about and that being queer wasn't bad, "But I can't make any money off of you." So, she dressed and left – with Jimmy sitting confused on the bed. After a minute, he left the room, the bar and walked slowly down the steps into the crowded city where he felt as alone – and at the same time, exposed –as he had ever been.

The call girl had not merely opened Jimmy's closet door: she kicked him out of it into a reality for which he was wholly unprepared. Jimmy had had a strict Catholic upbringing in a family that was observant to the point of being dogmatic – and there was no place in the religion or his family for a gay man. Jimmy also found himself in Ensign Johnson's shoes: a gay man in the Navy, forced to live a carefully concealed double life.

Soon, though, these two double lives would become one.

Two days out of Subic Bay heading towards Vietnam, several sailors, including Jimmy, were swabbing the deck. Ensign Johnson called out Jimmy and asked him quietly if he was alright, as he had seen a change in the sailor since his return from shore leave. When Jimmy said he was fine, Johnson persisted and ordered him to come to his quarters after mess.

Later that day, their conversation began with the ensign offering Jimmy a beer from an ice chest. The relaxed atmosphere helped to put Jimmy at ease, and he felt comfortable sharing his experience with the call girl. When he reached the end, he hesitated and said, "For some reason, I wasn't interested. At first, it upset me – but then I started thinking that I don't know who I am.

Johnson looked at him and said, "This worries you." Jimmy explained his Catholic upbringing, his religion's attitude towards homosexuals and, most of all, that he felt that he was going to be in trouble with God. "I'm sorry you feel that way," Johnson said. "You don't have to lie to anyone – I don't." Jimmy gave him a confused look.

Johnson explained that God made him and that he was exactly how God chose him to be – just as he had made him. He went on saying that neither he nor Jimmy were in trouble and that he understood Jimmy's dilemma, because he had faced it, too. "So, here we are together. Nobody has to lie in this room. Nobody has to feel anything but honest. And nobody is going to punish you for being honest."

Then the ensign asked Jimmy what he thought was an odd question: he asked about his ability to defend himself. Jimmy replied that he had done well in hand-to-hand combat, plus he had grown up with older brothers. Johnson said that he had been looking for a friend to "watch his back," which, again, seemed strange to Jimmy , since they were on board the Henrico with men much bigger than himself.

Before Jimmy could dwell on the question, Johnson added cautiously that he was looking for someone who felt the same as he did about male relationships. Jimmy stared at him and asked, "Are you asking me out on a date?" Johnson replied, "Yes – yes I am. And I hope that you're attracted to me the same way I am to you." Jimmy wasn't sure what or how to respond, saying that it was all new to him.

He added that he had always admired the ensign from afar as being a nice guy and that, because of the Navy's policy towards homosexuals, they should just get to know each other and see how it went from there. "I don't want to get into any trouble," he said.

Johnson put an affectionate hand on Jimmy's shoulder and told him that he was a past master at discretion. With that, he went over to his bunk, pulled off the bedspread and lifted up the mattress to reveal a hidden compartment underneath. He opened a hinged plywood door – inside was crammed cartons of cigarettes, bottles of booze and a plastic bag filled with rolled joints.

Jimmy had never tried marijuana, but was willing to try as Johnson lit one with his lighter and showed the neophyte the proper grass-smoking technique. He gave Jimmy the joint to try and Jimmy did well inhaling, but he coughed as he tried to hold it in his lungs. Soon, though, the high hit him and he found that he liked the feeling. The two men started laughing and joking as they smoked, drank more beer and talked about the ship, the crew and the chow. More importantly, Jimmy felt protected in Tom Johnson's presence.

It was a new and welcomed feeling.

36

Chapter 7 - Got You Now, Sailor Boy

THE HENRICO DOCKED in Da Nang, a major cargo port on the east coast of South Vietnam. The ship bustled with activity as support combat troops for the escalating Vietnam conflict filed down three gangplanks to the dock. Sailors stacked crates of food, medical supplies, ammunition and weapons onto large pallets. Crane operators swung the pallets to the dock. American sailors and GIs served as stevedores, loading the cargo onto waiting trucks with forklifts. On the ship's main deck, a group of sailors moved ammunition crates and supplies in wooden boxes. Jimmy and his buddies were among the group. Ensign Johnson watched them from the poop deck.

The sailors grumbled at the complaints. Jimmy heard them saying that he should come down and help them if he wanted to get things done faster. One of them muttered that Johnson didn't want to exhaust himself before he went chasing after male hustlers. Another grunted in agreement that he had heard that Johnson was bisexual and was seen ashore in the Phillippines with both the local whores and street boys. Jimmy listened and worked in silence.

The next day, one of the sailors on the work crew, a Seaman Fred Brown, questioned Jimmy about his conversation with the ensign. Jimmy evaded saying that all they discussed was some chores and if Jimmy would do him a favor by helping him carry gifts back to the ship. Brown warned Jimmy "to be careful with that guy – I heard he does some strange things. You don't want to get pulled into his web."

The next morning, the crew members scheduled for shore leave were in their dress white uniforms and assembled near the gangplank. While waiting for the officer of the watch to sound the dismissal whistle at 1030 hours, small groups of men chatted about their plans. Some of them, including Brown, asked Jimmy to go with them. Jimmy reminded the sailor that he was supposed to help the ensign. All of the men chuckled and left Jimmy alone when they were dismissed.

Ensign Johnson approached Jimmy and asked him if he was ready to go. Jimmy said yes and the two men went ashore to catch a cab into Da Nang.

Market Street in Da Nang was a bustling place. The narrow, wet street was crowded with shops and cafes. Taxi cabs, delivery trucks, motor scooters and bicycles advanced as quickly as they could along the cluttered roadway. Street vendors sold their goods from sidewalk carts with high-pitched, nasal calls. The air felt as if it could be wrung out like a towel; the street was redolent of old fried rice and dead fish. South Vietnamese Regulars, American sailors and GIs stood out conspicuously among the local shoppers.

Ensign Johnson and Jimmy studied brightly-colored shirts behind a store window. Johnson placed his arm on Jimmy's shoulder as they spoke. They looked in each other's eyes; a mutual feeling of trust and friendship was felt by both men. They smiled and walked down the noisy street. Their first destination was Frank Lin's pawn shop.

Jimmy was looking all around and in the store windows as they walked down the busy street. From within a doorway loomed the sallow face of a Vietnamese gangster named Pham Son-Tien. Pham Son-Tien was short, stocky, man with dark hair and eyes. He reached across the doorway and handed a cigarette to a large menacing

Vietnamese man, Dalat Trang. The two gangsters watched Johnson and Jimmy as they turned the corner and walked down the side street.

The sailors stopped in front of a store with a sign above the door that was written in Vietnamese, Chinese and English "Frank Lin's Pawn Shop – Highest Prices Paid." Two Chinese men stood outside the entrance of the pawn shop, watching Johnson and Jimmy walk toward them. Johnson explained that they were Mr. Lin's body guards, Jeffrey and Vincent.

Ci Wen Yang, a pretty Chinese woman in a red silk dress, welcomed the sailors with a smile and accented English. Johnson professed to being a friend of Mr. Lin's from his last trip to Vietnam. Shortly, the men were escorted into a large showroom filled with all types of musical instruments, power tools, jewelry, watches and cameras. Off to the rear was a large desk, chairs and a leather couch. Bookcases covered one wall.

Mr. Lin was a Taiwanese man with black, short hair. He wore glasses and dressed in a black suit with a red shirt, and his manner was extremely relaxed. Lin invited the men to sit. After Johnson introduced James Zappalorti and the usual perfunctory chit-chat took place, Johnson got down to his reason for being there.

"Frank," Johnson said, "I'd like to buy two Polaroid cameras, four gold rings and several good watches – that is if you have them available?" Mr. Lin said that business was slow and that he had plenty of supplies: a Vietnamese drug gang had moved into the area and was harassing his customers, including stealing from and killing at least one.

After making his purchases, Johnson held a ring up to Jimmy and asked if the young sailor liked it: it was a 14-karat gold crucifix that wrapped around the band. Jimmy took the ring from Johnson, put it on his right ring finger and looked at it admiringly. Jimmy was flattered.

Tom said, "It's yours. A gift for our friendship."

To celebrate the transactions, the young Chinese woman

produced a bottle of Vietnamese wine and three glasses on a tray. The wine bottle had a dead venomous bamboo viper snake coiled in it. Tradition had it that the spirit would bestow good health and virility upon the drinker.

Frank opened the bottle and poured the wine into three glasses, while Jimmy stared in shock at the snake that was soaking in the drink he was about to imbibe. The three men took their glasses, gently clicked them, took a sip and smiled at each other.

As they drank, Frank, addressing the ensign in a fatherly tone as "Tom," urged him to be particularly cautious on the way back to the ship. He said that the Vietnamese Son gang was not only ruthless, but had, in the past, followed some of his customers so that they could rob, beat and, again, kill them. Frank said, "I would not want this to happen to you and your friend."

Tom lifted his shirt to reveal a pistol. He boasted that he wasn't worried about a bunch of "street punks" and that he had Jimmy to watch his back. "They'll have to take what they want from my dead hand." Frank Lin warned Tom not to underestimate the gang, either in terms of their intelligence or their violence: they were organized, armed and traveled in groups. The young woman handed the ensign a leather pack that concealed the items he purchased and wished him a safe journey back to the Henrico.

Night had fallen by the time the two Americans had concluded their business with Frank Lin. They made their way back to the busy street market and the local red light district Prostitutes walked the street and openly approached the dozens of U.S. servicemen and South Vietnamese soldiers. Others loitered in the alleys or went in and out of the establishments with uniformed men. Music blared from radios; there was an uninterrupted babble of drunken voices.

As Jimmy and Tom continued down the street, Pham and his three thugs followed them from a distance. The two sailors walked past a butcher shop that sold dogs. Jimmy watched the proceedings with a sick fascination. Farther along Market Street, they stopped to watch a snake charmer perform. At one point, he reached into his basket and pulled out a cobra. The man proceeded to cut the snake lengthwise and drained the blood into several glasses lined up on a table, mixing it with equal parts of rye whiskey. Buyers lined up for a glass of the mixture and Tom told Jimmy that the belief was that, like with many other such concoctions, this potion was not only a curative but ensured extra-potent erections.

Jimmy was skeptical.

Tom said, well, there's only one way to find out. He handed the charmer some money, grabbed two glasses of the bloody cocktail and handed one to Jimmy. Tom gulped it down in one shot and grinned saying, boy, that was good! Jimmy, not wanting to be outdone, cautiously drained his glass. Tom then reached into his leather backpack and pulled out a wad of money and handed it to the man who carefully studied it. When he was satisfied, he handed Tom a spoon filled with a white powder. The ensign rubbed a finger full on his gums and smiled with approval. The charmer took Tom's pack, put two large wrapped packages inside and tossed the pack back to him. Jimmy watched not understanding the transaction.

However, Pham Son-Tien did – and he continued to watch the two sailors, as did his bodyguard, Dalat Trang, his brother, Long Son-Tien, and another dangerous looking man, Phnom Penh.

Unaware that they were being followed, Tom suggested that they celebrate their friendship in the Silk Dragon, an establishment with private rooms. As they walked along, they came across a show featuring three scantily-clad transvestites in dresses, heels and makeup on a platform, dancing and flirting with passersby. Tom and Jimmy stopped in front of the makeshift stage and watched the show. The ensign threw a kiss to one of the dancers, who immediately descended the stage to dance with him. The performer kissed Johnson, who slipped some money into her hand.

Jimmy stared at the dancers in confusion and asked Tom, "Are they men or women?" In answer, the performer took took Jimmy's hand and shoved it between her legs. Shocked at feeling a penis, Jimmy quickly pulled his hand back. Tom laughed and said, "Let's get to the Silk Dragon and get a room before the cobra blood wears off."

The Silk Dragon was a rundown hotel, restaurant and drinking establishment filled with prostitutes. Some of them nursed babies. The barstools and tables were crowded. Several couples danced on the wooden floor. Most of the patrons eating and drinking were Vietnamese, but there were also some American military personnel mixed in the crowd.

Tom was greeted by Madam Xiong, a Vietnamese woman close to fifty and wearing a dress that exposed her breasts almost to the nipples. Tom returned the greeting, and when she asked if his companion was also in the navy, Tom quipped that his friend was an admiral. After the pleasantries, he ordered clean sheets, fried shrimp and a case of beer, and led Jimmy to Room Five, where they removed their shoes and got comfortable listening to music on a radio.

As they relaxed, Madam Xiong was busy transacting with the gangster Pham and his compatriots. Satisfied with the fee, Madam Xiong gave the men the room number for the two sailors, as well as enough information to let them appear to be part of her staff.

From the hallway came a knock and a voice. "Room service. I have your dinner," said Long Son-Tien. Johnson looked in the peephole and saw a waiter with a tray of food. Tom opened the door and pointed to the table. Long Son-Tien placed the tray down and started arranging the plates on the table. Jimmy came out of the bathroom and grabbed his bottle of beer.

With slow, obsequious movements, Long Son-Tien asked if everything was to Tom's liking. The ensign said yes, handed him a five-dollar bill as a tip and asked him to lock the door on the way out.

As the gangster opened the door to leave, the rest of the gang pushed their way into the room with drawn weapons. Tom quickly realized that his gun was across the room and out of reach. Regardless, he was still a sailor and angrily demanded who they were and what they wanted.

Ignoring Tom, Pham Son-Tien ordered neither man to move. Dalat Trang produced handcuffs for Johnson, and Long Son-Tien had a rope to tie Jimmy. When the gang members got close enough, Tom immediately went into action. He grabbed Dalat and flipped him over his head right into Phnom and Long. Pham quickly moved into the scuffle, punching Tom in the side of his head with a fist braced with brass knuckles and then slamming him stomach first onto the bed. Dalat recovered, knelt on Tom's back, pulled his arms together and handcuffed his wrists.

"Keep your hands off me!" Jimmy yelled as he kicked Phnom between the legs, dropping him in pain. Meanwhile, Long knocked Jimmy senseless with a wooden club. He fell to the floor as the other two men tied his hands and feet with rope, leaving him lying senseless on the floor next to an easy chair

Pham snarled at Johnson, who gasped with pain. He accused the sailors of being "faggot drug dealers" who had invaded his territory. A stern lesson would be taught.

Pham said, "Sailor, you like to take it in the ass? Remove his pants. We will use him like a woman." The men removed Tom's pants and undershorts as he lay across the bed on his stomach, clad only in his white tee-shirt.

Long took the wooden club and forced it into Tom's rectum, pumping it in and out as the ensign screamed in pain. Once Long was done, he handed the club to Phnom, who brutally rammed it almost five-inches deep into Tom. He pulled out the blood and flesh covered stick and waved around to everyone's laughter while Tom lay moaning on the bed.

Phnom returned to assaulting Tom and continued doing so until he said he was tired. "Someone take over for me." Dalat grabbed the club.

All the while, Jimmy was lying on the floor regaining his senses and watching and hearing his friend being raped. The gangsters were too distracted to pay any attention to Jimmy, who, hardly daring to breathe, struggled to loosen the rope around his wrists.

Tom was still not broken and yelled out obscenities and spat at his attackers. Pham said deliberately, "For that you will suffer even more." He took a pair of white rubber gloves from a leather sack and put them on. Then he grabbed a straight razor from the same sack and said to his men, "Stand him up now. He will no longer be able to sodomize other men!"

Pham grabbed Tom's penis in his left hand and, with one quick motion of the razor, cut it off. Tom screamed while Pham held it up and smiled. Mutilated, bleeding and in agony, Tom, with his last bit of strength, kicked Pham squarely in the groin. Pham doubled over in pain, dropping the razor and Tom's penis.

Jimmy struggled with maniacal strength until the rope slipped off of his wrists. He quickly untied his feet and stood up. Not noticing Jimmy, and insulted and furious by Tom's unexpected blow, Pham pulled out a .38-caliber revolver, put it to Tom's head and fired a single, point-blank shot.

Ensign Tom Johnson's forehead exploded. The gunshot's momentum threw body backwards, onto the bed, where he silently gazed at the ceiling.

Jimmy, standing behind the easy chair, watched in disbelief as his friend died. Jimmy dashed across the room toward the door dressed only in his t-shirt and bloodied Navy white pants, while the four gang members stood mesmerized by the gore of Johnson's body.

When Tom's killers realized that Jimmy was making a break, they unsuccessfully tried to stop him as he passed through the unlocked door and into the hallway. Chasing after him, Dalat was the first to grab him; but Jimmy elbowed him in the face, knocking him to the floor and temporarily obstructing the others. This gave Jimmy the time to get to the window.

Knowing that a bullet to the head would be worse than being cut by the broken glass, Jimmy dove through the window leading with his elbows to protect his face. Luckily, it was only a one-floor drop to the alley below. Jimmy broke his fall with his arms. Blood dripped from his face and hands onto his white tee-shirt. He stood dizzily and staggered toward the crowded main street.

With Pham shouting, "Get him! He must not escape!"

Phnom Penh, club in hand, leapt out the window in pursuit.

He caught up to Jimmy within a few steps and whacked him on the back of the head, sending Jimmy to the pavement. Dalat and the newly arrived Long viciously kicked Jimmy as he tried to rise from the ground. The torrent of punches and kicks knocked him back down – that's when Pham arrived and brandished his pistol.

Jimmy was already beaten half to death when Pham rolled his head backwards and aimed the .38 between his eyes. Jimmy squinted, waiting to die. Pham shot two bullets over his head and said, Oh, you're gonna die alright – but just which shot gonna do it?" He grinned at Jimmy. "I think this next bullet. A bullet…just for you, queer boy!"

As Pham aimed once more, a Navy Shore Patrol Jeep drove past the Silk Dragon. Three Shore Patrol Officers, Brady, Jenkins and O'Riley, rode in the vehicle and had been engaged in conversation about their girlfriends back home. Officer Jenkins happened to glance down the alley as they drove past. He saw four men standing over a bloody U.S. sailor.

"Stop, Charlie!" Jenkins shouted. "One of our guys is getting beaten back there! Officer O' Riley immediately stopped the Jeep at the edge of the alley. The officers pulled their .45s and jumped out. Officer Jenkins pointed his handgun at the gang and ordered them sharply to put their hands up.

Pham defiantly screamed back, "Fuck you, sailor boys! Dalat and the other gang members moved in a threatening manner toward the three Shore Patrol Officers. Jenkins did not hesitate; he shot Pham in the arm. Dalat, Long, and Phnom immediately dropped their weapons and went against one wall. Brady did the cuffing.

While O'Riley called for backup and an ambulance, Jimmy struggled up. "They killed my friend, Tom Johnson!" he labored through a mangled mouth. "He's up there, in Room Five." Officer Jenkins surveyed Jimmy's wounds, "You ain't in such good shape yourself. If we hadn't driven past the alley when we did, who knows what would have happened." He jerked his head heavenward. "Someone up there must really like you."

Chapter 8 - Be Very Gentle With Him

JIMMY'S "LUCKY STREAK" continued when an ambulance happened to be nearby – he was inside and being tended to within five minutes. Roughly five minutes after that, the South Vietnamese Police arrived at the scene. They arrested Pham and his three other gang members for murder and robbery.

The ambulance took Jimmy to a military hospital. What followed was an investigation of Ensign Johnson's murder and a cursory look into the circumstances of the homosexual affair between the two sailors. The Navy then closed their files with its usual circumspection and Jimmy was sent back to the States and hospitalized.

Ensign Tom Johnson was dead. The Jimmy Zappalorti who stepped off the USS Henrico hours before was also dead. He had watched the savage sexual assault, mutilation and murder of his friend. He had been brutally beaten and narrowly escaped death.

For Jimmy, the file would never be closed: it would be a wound that would remain open and never heal.

He was forever changed.

The Navy did not inform the Zappalorti family of the events in Da Nang. All they knew was that Jimmy's letters home stopped without explanation. Frantic with worry, Mary and Michael repeatedly contacted the Navy for information, but they were initially ignored.

Finally, Mary contacted the American Red Cross for their help. After two weeks, the organization found Jimmy in a military hospital in Philadelphia, Pennsylvania. Mike called the hospital and made arrangements to go see Jimmy. Philadelphia was only a three-hour drive from Staten Island and, except for Bobby, who couldn't get the day off from his job working at the Staten Island Zoo, the entire Zappalorti family piled into their car to visit Jimmy.

When they arrived, they were directed to the third floor, where they gathered in the hallway outside of Jimmy's room. Doctor Morris, a Navy physician, apprised the family of Jimmy's condition.

"I want to be very straight with you folks," the doctor said. "James has had a serious nervous breakdown." In softened terms, he related the entire story of Tom and Jimmy's attack. "He's had the kind of severe mental and physical trauma that few people ever get over," the doctor said. "Your son and brother is in a bad mental state. You all have to be very gentle with him."

The family was just beginning to process Jimmy's condition, both in terms of the present and the future, when Dr. Morris added, "There is more I have to tell you. Did you know that your son is a homosexual?

Mike deflated. The rest of the family reeled as if struck by a giant fist.

"No way," Mike blurted. "That's bullshit!"

"It doesn't make sense," Mickey said.

"In high school he dated girls! He dated Dottie Hail and Dolores Cummings," Peggy remembered.

Mary looked at the doctor and demanded, "Did he tell you this?"

The nodded his head. "Keeping this secret has been tearing him up. He can't deal with it right now. So, if you want your son back, your brother back, you have to understand this. Help him."

Mary brushed by the doctor and walked into Jimmy's room. Her son was sitting on the bed appearing much older than when she last saw him. Jimmy looked at his mother – she paused for a moment and then ran over and threw her arms around him. They hugged and cried. Mike, Mickey and Peggy soon entered and one by one took their turn hugging him. His father was the last.

Mary asked everybody to join hands. She began to pray and the rest of the family joined in.

At the time, with the armed services drafting all eligible young men, Jimmy's service was deemed exceptional and it was important that the Navy recognize his voluntary service to his country during wartime. In time, after the usual bureaucratic delays, Jimmy was granted veteran's benefits. The Navy gave Jimmy an Honorable Discharge and he returned home to Staten Island.

Mary called Bobby and told him about their visit. He came by as soon as he could.

"How's Jimmy doing?" Bobby asked. Mike shrugged. "He's recovered okay from the beating they gave him. He needed twenty-five stitches to close all the cuts on his hands, arms and face. The cuts healed months ago. They're not what I'm concerned with. Jimmy's psychiatrist told your mother and me that he was not only severely beaten but is also suffering from an emotional disability. But Bobby, there's more bad news…"

"What is it, Dad?" Bobby asked.

His father's face twisted into an expression of embarrassment. "How do I say this?" he said, looking for words. "Your brother… uh…he likes men. He's queer!"

Bobby was incredulous. "He is? What about his girlfriends in high school?"

"Think back," his father said, "they never lasted long." He shook his head and moaned, "My youngest son a queer! Bobby – you know what this means to me? I'll be disgraced! What will our friends and neighbors think of us?!"

Feeling far more upset for Jimmy than his father, Robert said, "Jimmy is still your son and my brother. Just because he likes men won't change that. Our family – our true friends and neighbors – will accept him. If they don't…then who cares what they think?"

Mike again shook his head. "Having a gay son is hard for me to accept, but I guess it will all work out." He put his arm around his son's shoulders and said, "Come on, let's go in the house. Your mother and Jimmy will be happy to see you! Robert and his father walked up the four cement steps and into the front door of the Zappalorti home.

Mike, Mary and Jimmy's siblings approached his homosexuality in their own ways.

Mary convinced herself that Jimmy's sexual preference was her fault – that there was something wrong with the way she raised him, that she had coddled him too much and let him stay close to the family where he was the most comfortable.

Mike saw Jimmy's homosexuality as a reflection on himself as a father, and it took years for him to accept the fact that his youngest son was a gay man. His struggle was intensified by his strong Roman Catholic faith, a faith that passionately condemned homosexuality. For years, Mike held a silent inner resentment toward Jimmy that came out in other ways: short-temperedness, finding fault with Jimmy's work, condemning Jimmy's staying out late at night and complaining about his coming into work late in the morning.

Despite the church's position on the subject, Mike and Mary found some comfort in speaking with their parish priest about Jimmy. Mike ultimately reflected back on the prejudice he had endured as an immigrant and this helped him along the path of accepting his son. All he had ever wanted was the best for him, for all of his children. In the end, Mike loved Jimmy as his son first – everything else came second.

Mickey loved Jimmy as his youngest brother and friend, and treated him as he always had in the past. "Jimmy was like my shadow, he was always around," Mickey often said. After himself being

Honorably Discharged from the Navy, Mickey came back home to work in the family stained glass business.

A big, deep-voiced man, Mickey kept his feelings to himself – a tendency that hid a good heart. He was often intimidating to strangers, but he always treated people well. Mickey was a talented partner in the stained glass business and his father's right hand man. He took Jimmy under his wing and taught him how to make stained glass windows.

But most of all, there was Jimmy. Actually, there were two; and they lived two separate lives in two different cities. First, there was the Jimmy who worked on Staten Island in his family's stained glass business. He was hard working, religious and sober. Then there was the Jimmy who fled to New York City's Greenwich Village where he could be a carefree gay man among people who accepted him for who he was. For the first Jimmy, the real world intruded upon his ability to be the second Jimmy: oversleeping and showing up for work late or not at all, which only increased his father's anger towards him.

Living a double life was not like turning a switch off and on. He could flee to the Village, but "Staten Island" always followed him in the form of his Catholic upbringing and its – and his own self – condemnation. Jimmy could find temporary forgetfulness in bottles of Budweiser; but once the liquid amnesia wore off, he was back having to confront his conflict with his homosexuality.

From childhood to the present, Catholicism had driven into his head the fact that he was a sinner for being attracted to men. But this only begged a larger question that has and continues torture gay believers: If God loves all of His creations, then how can only one kind of love be acceptable? Jimmy heard over and over again how God created human beings in His image. If that was the case then, based on Church doctrine, the "logical" conclusion was that homosexuals were not human beings.

Nonetheless, Jimmy continued to attend Mass, go to confession and say the Act of Contrition. He sincerely believed in God and prayed to Him whenever he was troubled. Sometimes his parents heard Jimmy crying at night in his room. Whether it was from nightmares, painful memories of his Navy experiences or from his inner turmoil, Jimmy kept the reasons to himself. He did not trouble his parents with the reasons behind his tears – and if truth be known, they were relieved.

Despite the inner and outer conflicts and tears, being back home among his family did help him. Working again with stained glass took his mind off his traumatic experience and gave him purpose. Jimmy also started gardening and cutting grass around town. But it was in the summer of 1967 that Jimmy found his refuge and his home: the beach on the Arthur Kill River.

He spent almost all of his free time there, cleaning the beach, swimming and crabbing using the rowboat given to him by a kindly neighbor, Charlie Kosa. For Jimmy, it was the place that would serve as the bookends of a new life that began – and would end – with tragedy.

In 1969, Jimmy began building a shack on the beach. It was a long, slow process, because all of the material and supplies he used to build the shack had to be carried down to the beach by hand or in a wheelbarrow. There was a sand road, but Jimmy had never learned to drive.

Jimmy nestled his "beach house" beneath a century-old red maple tree, built primarily from scrap lumber and plywood his father gave him. He also used old church window frames and installed plexiglass in them. The shingled roof was supported with four-by-four beams and half-inch plywood.

Throughout the spring and summer of 1970, and over the course of the next few summers, Jimmy built his beachside refuge.

The shack had two rooms. The first was a bedroom with a clear stained glass bay window facing the Outerbridge Crossing and the Arthur Kill River. Much of the furniture was discarded – things that he found about the neighborhood. Jimmy had a queen-sized bed, a nightstand with an oil lamp and ashtray on it, a large bookcase that held pictures of family and friends, and a rug on the plywood floor. A larger room served as a combined kitchen and living room, and lay just beyond the front entrance. This room was furnished with a table, chairs, couch, end tables and two more large bookcases.

Jimmy was able to get around the lack of running water for bathing by simply going the short distance to his parents' house to shower and shave; but he couldn't dash home every time he had to go the the bathroom. The solution was a small outhouse: He dug a six-foot hole in the gravelly sand, fashioned a wooden platform with a round hole in the center, placed a five-gallon bucket with the bottom removed over the hole and put an old toilet seat on the top on which to sit. Jimmy framed his do-it-yourself latrine with three plywood walls, a door and a pitched roof.

The finishing touches on the sanctuary were made on the outside. Jimmy hung an old chandelier in the red maple tree, just above the brick patio he built. He made a barbecue from cement blocks and bricks on which he cooked hamburgers and hot dogs when he entertained his friends. Jimmy also made a small wooden dock on the river to which he tied his rowboat.

In the summer, he would sit on the dock reading. He especially favored National Geographic magazines and mystery novels. Two stairs leading down to the beach were created with planks set on tree roots and two wrought-iron railings. By contrast, winters on the river could be frigid, so Jimmy fitted the shack with a small, glass-fronted, kerosene-burning stove The old appliance gave off plenty of heat and offered Jimmy the illusion of a fireplace, making his ramshackle cabin warm and comfortable. Jimmy would sometimes just sit and stare at the red, orange and blue flames of the kerosene stove as his mind drifted off to some faraway place he wanted to visit.

The trash that drifted in from the river offended his sense of order and cleanliness, so he always cleaned the beach and used what he could to build his shack, especially the driftwood. He neatly raked the flotsam and jetsam that washed up on the beach into neat piles that he picked up and carted away in his wheelbarrow.

Ultimately, the project absorbed Jimmy's interest and free time for over fifteen-years, because he was always improving upon the structure to make it just the way he wanted it.

In retrospect, Jimmy's shack was an apt metaphor for his life after the Navy: Making order from disorder, turning the discarded into something wanted and needed, and being able to exert power over his own world within a larger world that sought to take it away. Where others might have simply retreated into a hard shell, Jimmy was actively fighting for a purpose, for dignity, for fulfillment. The shack gave him all of those things.

But for all of the personal empowerment, it was also a source of refuge. The shack gave Jimmy an equal sense of comfort and of being away from his personal problems: Yes, he built it out of his own need for independence, but also to avoid tensions with his father.

Jimmy built a private place for reflection that was serviceable, but not fancy. In a sense, it was not built for beauty, because Jimmy did not feel wholly beautiful; nor did anyone around him think of him that way. Jimmy found his beauty by looking out rather than in. At the end of the day, he could watch the sun set over the river and; at night, the lights on the Outerbridge Crossing were his earthly stars.

Chapter 9 - Jimmy's Life in Charleston

JIMMY'S RECOVERY FROM his nervous breakdown was slow. When he was strong enough, he started to help out with the family stained glass business. The Zappalorti business name soon reflected the addition of personnel: "Michael and Sons Stained Glass Studio." Mike wanted Bobby to join Mickey and Jimmy in the business, but his middle son's interests and passions were music and studying reptiles and amphibians – ultimately, he became a herpetologist.

Still, there was a huge change in Jimmy's personality, from the person who went to war to the person who returned: depressed, reserved, quiet and with few close friends. He kept himself busy by learning to make stained glass windows with his father and brothers and, though a slow learner, but with practice he eventually caught on to the craft.

On weekends he sought bottled relief: wine and beer. Never belligerent or morose while sober or drunk, Jimmy instead became silly, funny and boisterous. But it was what played inside Jimmy's head and which he rarely shared – memories from Vietnam – contributed not only to depression, but to what can only be called regression: He became childlike, innocent and naive, sometimes to the point of acting delusional.

Drinking on weekends became a habit, and when he drank too much he would indulge in grandiose fantasies, such as being related to the Queen of England or the Rockefellers. He rambled on about owning controlling stock in ConEd or that he owned the Empire State Building. How he came to believe these delusional ideas was never quite clear to his parents or brothers and sister. When they tried to tell Jimmy that he was wrong, he became boisterous, argumentative and more insistent that he indeed was related to Queen Elizabeth and could prove it through his family ancestry. However, the next day when he slept off the alcohol that fogged his thinking, he could not remember saying any of the whimsical things about which he had argued the night before.

When not in New York or working in the family business, he spent his time keeping the family home, inside and out, clean and orderly. As with his beach house, Jimmy was able to exert a control over his immediate environment that he couldn't over so many other aspects of his life, both past and present. Jimmy gladly worked in the family backyard. In the spring he would plant flowers, cut the grass, rake the yard and keep the grounds neat and clean. He also helped his mother in the house, vacuuming, cooking, and washing dirty clothes. Gradually, he took over the housekeeping chores as Mary's health declined.

As the years passed, Jimmy's confidence slowly grew and he extended his "sphere of control." He helped his neighbors on Androvette Street in kind, unobtrusive ways: picking up trash; collecting soda and beer bottles and placing them in garbage cans; sweeping the street; clipping hedges; and cutting lawns. Sometimes he would get paid for these services; sometimes he did it for free. The drone of pushing an old-fashioned lawn mower was soothing to his nerves; the simple back-and-forth movements made him feel needed and useful.

In the summer, the Knights of Columbus, who owned the property next door to the Zappalortis, held picnics in their large yard. Jimmy was hired to clean and rake the trash. He also compulsively and good-naturedly cleaned the rest of Androvette Street. It was common to see Jimmy hiking all over Charleston, picking up trash, bottles and beer cans as he went, and placing them in garbage cans along the street. More than one resident thanked him for his efforts.

Longtime neighbors and friends, such as the Kosa and Reiter families, had known Jimmy since childhood and accepted him as a gentle soul. Owen Reiter, in a newspaper interview shortly after the murder, said of Jimmy, "[He] was a neighbor, who did neighborly things. When I first moved here I had two young boys, a son and a stepson, who were both twelve years old. People said, 'Aren't you concerned with your kids, playing in the woods and whatnot with a gay man around?' It was well known that Jimmy was no threat to the kids in Charleston. On the contrary, he looked out for them and played with them. Most kids liked Jimmy. Jimmy would tell my kids, 'Don't go out in the rowboat without your father around.' He treated them like a parent, like a responsible adult."

Eventually, everyone knew Jimmy – especially his signature seasonal attire. On hot summer days, he often wore sandals and short, cut-off jeans and t-shirts, the latter of which always showed off his belly. In winter, which he hated, his usual uniform was long underwear, dungarees and a long-sleeve shirt with a wool sweater over it, white socks and biker boots. He also sported a leather jacket, gloves and wool scarf. Some of his outfits were eye catching because of the bright colors he wore, but when he went to church he dressed more conservatively.

In December of 1965, Mary's younger sister, Regina Ryan, gave the Zappalorti family a brand new upright piano as a Christmas present. This was a wonderful gift, as Mary also loved playing music on her father's concertina. Now she could develop her skills on the piano keys, and gave herself lessons by reading piano music books. Eventually, she became a fairly good musician.

His mother's inspiration made Jimmy wanted to learn to play the piano, too; but he didn't have the patience or concentration to practice from books or to learn to read music. Instead, Bobby showed Jimmy a few chords and melodies on the piano, and the rest he picked up on his own. Jim Anderson, who was the lead singer and guitar player in Bobby's band, also gave Jimmy some pointers. Jimmy also had time to practice during work: with the Zappalorti stained glass business' major customers being churches in all five boroughs, Jimmy always had lunchtime access to a piano or organ.

Jimmy threw himself at and into music. With many hours of practice (to the point that he almost drove Mike and Mary crazy) Jimmy learned to play the piano by ear. Jimmy plucked out the notes on the keys by trial and error, then played them over and over, and eventually memorized tunes. With many years of practice, he eventually mastered a large repertoire of songs. He also played his grandfather Tom Ryan's concertina. Jimmy's favorite musical entertainer was the flamboyant Liberace, who he emulated and admired.

Soon he was entertaining family and friends, as well as crossing the Hudson to play in clubs in New York.

Chapter 10 - Jimmy and Greenwich Village

JIMMY LOVED GOING into New York City and being in Greenwich Village. He liked the people, all the little art shops, clothing stores, and the gay bars. He felt accepted there and made friends with many shop owners, bartenders and gay people who hung out in the Village. Jimmy used to go to a bookshop on Bleeker Street where he found a book about the history of Greenwich Village and its people. He purchased it and read it from cover to cover. He learned many interesting things about the Village, which gave him something to talk about with his friends. Jimmy liked that the 1970's were the heyday of the Gay Liberation Movement in New York City. Influenced by the Gay Community and what he learned about their movement, Jimmy slowly accepted his own homosexuality.

The mantra of the gay movement was: "Come out" of the closet and declare your homosexuality with pride. The reasoning was that since homosexuality could be hidden or disguised, gays could always be mistreated, put upon, marginalized and beaten unless they asserted their identity and accepted their place in American society. If they remained "invisible, gays would always be kicked around," Randy Shilts later wrote in his book about the AIDS crisis, "because they would never assert their power." Coming out meant risking one's neck, one's family, job, home, freedom, and a great many other factors, but the rewards were real and tangible. It was something any gay person would consider. It meant accepting one's self-identity, setting a new honest relationship with oneself and others, and joining in with courageous friends. Once out, it gave each individual a political stake in trying to change the attitudes and rules of society and in continuing the Gay Pride Movement. As more and more joined in, they found new safety within their numbers and new friends. The combined Gay Movement became a political voting force that politicians eventually took notice.

In 1970, the first gay liberation marches were held in New York and Los Angeles. Later in the decade, the first openly gay candidates were elected to Congress and various city councils, such as Barney Frank from Massachusetts. In December 1973 the American Psychiatric Association voted to remove homosexuality from its official list of mental disorders. The 1970's were also a time of gay promiscuity, sometimes taken to extremes. The three large cities of Los Angeles, San Francisco and New York (where AIDS would first erupt in the next decade) each had dozens of gay bars, discos and bathhouses, where anonymous sexual contacts went on day and night.

The new gay visibility, sexuality and openness provoked a backlash from right wing fundamentalists and others, such as from Anita Bryant in 1977. The backlash continued into the 1980's, when the AIDS epidemic seemed to "prove" to many the consequences of the "sin" of homosexuality. The Metropolitan Community Church (MCC) was founded by Troy Perry in 1968 after he was excommunicated from his Pentecostal ministry for being homosexual. MCC was the first Protestant church to openly cater to gays, lesbians, bisexuals and transgendered people and their friends. Three different MCC churches were set on fire in 1973. One MCC minister was brutally murdered, stabbed thirteen times and slashed across his throat. The church that was started in Perry's West Hollywood apartment living room now has 314 congregations and over 52,000 members, in 16 different countries.

Radical new gay rights groups sprang up, such as ACT UP, to keep AIDS from claiming more lives in silence, without public sympathy or government support. President Ronald Reagan never mentioned the nationwide healthcare crisis until late in his second term, after the autoimmune disease had spread to heterosexuals. ACT UP tactics included Azaps," which was a method of sending noisy protesters to interrupt Catholic Church services, which alienated many people against them. Cardinal John O'Connor, was a frequent target of the group ACT UP, and was often criticized for not supporting gay rights issues. When Cardinal O'Connor invited Joseph Cardinal Ratzinger to speak at St. Peter's Church in 1988, eight ACT UP activists in the church leaped up and shouted slurs like "Nazi!" "Anti-Christ!" and "Stop the Inquisition!" The eight ACT UP members were asked to leave the church for disrupting the service. John Cardinal Ratzinger became the new Pope and leader of the Roman Catholic Church after the death of Pope John Paul II in 2005.

In June of 1973, an unknown arsonist (or arsonists), who were never caught, lit a fire under the stairs of the Upstairs Bar, a gay gathering place in New Orleans. The ensuing firestorm killed thirty-two people. One victim, a schoolteacher, was notified that he was fired from his job while he was still in intensive care for burns. He died two weeks later. This New Orleans tragedy was almost completely ignored by the press, politicians, and even churches in the area. Some families refused to collect the remains of their dead children. The MCC church stepped in and gave them a proper Christian burial.

In 1980, a 38-year-old former New York Transit Authority policeman opened fire with a machine gun outside a New York City gay bar called The Ramrod. This was a night club that Jimmy often went to on weekends to meet his gay friends. He would wear his gold shirt, black pants, black boots and black leather jacket in keeping with the dress code of the bar. Luckily, Jimmy was not at The Ramrod on the night of this horrible incident. Two gay men were killed and six others were wounded by the machine gun bullets that were fired by a homophobic man. Street gangs in Seattle, Washington roamed the city parks and beat gay men with baseball bats in 1983. One gang raped two gay men with a crowbar. When arrested, a gang member told police, "If we don't kill these fags, they'll kill us with their fucking AIDS disease." AIDS unfortunately became a justification for violence by the ignorant, a pseudo-reason to provoke unreasonable human beings. By the time the actor Rock Hudson died of complications from AIDS in 1985, the general public began to take notice. It was a double shock to many in the public because the handsome, deep-voiced actor had always played virile, heterosexual, female love-interest males on television and in the movies. By 1985, 12,000 other Americans were also infected with or had died from the so called "gay plague."

Jimmy was fond of the colors gold and silver. At home and in his shack, he would decorate his favorite pieces of furniture by trimming them with gold and silver paint. He had a way of making old things look neat and clean by dressing them up this way. The wrought-iron railing of the house, the mailbox, the flag pole, even the edges of the bricks on the path of the house, all ended up being painted silver and gold. In 1982, Jimmy bought himself a cuckoo clock at an antique store in Greenwich Village. It worked really well, but its wood finish was badly tarnished, so he easily remedied that. Jimmy painted it silver and gold and hung it in the family living room. He loved that clock, and would show it off to anyone who visited the house. He would push the hands around to the top of the hour, so the bird would pop out and sing, "Cuckoo! Cuckoo!"

Another special time piece that Jimmy purchased in 1984, at a shop in the Village was an antiquated French provincial-style clock. It was the old-fashion type that he had to wide-up with a key. On the hour the clock chimed loudly. He kept the clock on his bedroom dresser because he liked the tone. Between the chime of the French clock in his room and the cuckoo clock in the living room, the house echoed with interesting sounds on an hourly basis.

Jimmy's innate drive and simple human need for love and sex eventually forced him away from the conservative Staten Island. He learned to make a long and complicated commute on New York City buses or the Staten Island Rapid Transit train, to the Staten Island Ferry, and then on the New York subway system, to visit the gay bars and neighborhoods of Greenwich Village in Manhattan. There, he found companionship and warm acceptance.

Greenwich Village is a neighborhood of about four square miles, from the Hudson River east to Broadway and from Houston Street north to 14th Street. Although it is on the same island and within the same borough as the rest of Manhattan, it has a unique character all its own and has been bohemian from its earliest history. When the Dutch bought Manhattan Island from the Indians in 1626, Greenwich Village was a woodland teeming with timber rattlesnakes, bobcat, deer, elk, owls, wild turkey and lots of other wildlife native to New York State. Sapokanican Indians lived in a small village along the Hudson River and fished for trout and striped bass. Then the British took over.

The secluded nature of Greenwich Village changed dramatically during a series of smallpox, yellow fever and cholera epidemics in 1799, 1803, 1805 and 1821. Thousands of immigrants living in overcrowded areas to the south and east tried to escape contagion by moving into hastily constructed housing in the West Village. The apartments built for the newcomers were constructed along narrow twisting lanes that followed the contours of the old farms, Indian trails, cow paths and the rerouted Minetta Brook. These meandering roads and smaller-scale buildings set Greenwich Village apart from the rigid grid pattern of taller buildings in the core of Manhattan.

The new influx included German, Irish, and Italian immigrants. They joined a shrinking but established upper class, and resident dissidents of many types who called themselves bohemians. The largely Catholic newcomers and the Aold money" set were both repelled by the bohemian free-love advocates, intellectuals, writers, and artists of all kinds. Gradually the more tolerant types were attracted and stayed and most of the intolerant moved elsewhere.

Most major American cities have their own community of bohemian types along with their underground gathering places. The anonymity of the big city has always attracted those who did not fit in with conventional morality. Some bohemians discreetly accepted "Lavender Lads" and "Isle of Lesbos" women into their midst beginning in the 1890's, although they were still ostracized and subject to persecution. Certain streets, dance halls, or beer gardens in Greenwich Village became known hangouts. By the 1920's Greenwich Village attracted even more dissidents who advocated unconventional behavior, including sexual behavior. Feminists of the early 20th century fueled the bohemian fervor in Greenwich Village. They were emancipated, free-spirited, independent and fierce champions of women's suffrage and rights. Coffee shops, cafés, restaurants, clubs, art galleries, libraries and theaters sprang up to serve the needs of all the Villagers.

In the early days of Prohibition, speakeasies and lesbian tearooms (they served whiskey in teacups to thwart licensing laws) became the first gay bars before the term was invented. The bohemians, anarchists, socialists and intellectuals of the 1920's and 1930's were replaced by beatnik poets and method actors in the 1950's. In turn, the beatniks were replaced by rock-and-rollers, pop artists, civil rights activists and anti-war activists in the 1960's. As many authors and journalists have observed, Greenwich Village is not so much a place in New York as it is a "state of mind."

A *Life* magazine story in 1963 told of a colony of homosexuals in

Greenwich Village. The article drew young gay men from all over the country, many of them isolated in stifling small towns. The evolution continues, as New York is a living, constantly changing city.

By 1967, state courts in New York, New Jersey and Pennsylvania all had acknowledged the legal right of homosexuals to gather in a public bar. Yet, in 1968 the laws of New York State had only changed again slightly.

The New York Appellate Division ruled that "close dancing" between same-sex couples was legal and that merely serving liquor to homosexuals did not constitute running a "disorderly house." Court changes came faster than changes in the virulently homophobic New York City Police Department, since there remained vague laws against "lewd and indecent behavior" or "solicitation" on the books. In fact, the loosening of restrictions provoked a police backlash. Vice squads could and did burst into a tavern and arrest patrons at their own whim. Police raids were so frequent that gay bars led a gypsy existence and opened and closed frequently.

There was a mayoral race in 1969, which was typically a time when the incumbent wanted to show that he was tough on crime. Incumbent Mayor John Lindsay especially needed to show he was for law and order, as the entire nation was convulsed in civil rights riots, protests against the Vietnam War, demonstrations for Black Panthers, for women's liberation, and the entire counterculture movement. Men who grew their hair long were once considered effeminate. Now the Along-haired hippie freaks" did so to show their defiance of authority. In 1975, the Gay Pride movement was in its early days, fueled by the "Stonewall Uprising," which was a landmark event in gay history. A New York State Liquor Authority law that dated from the 1930's banned any bar or restaurant from serving liquor to gay men or lesbians. Establishments that did so were defined as "disorderly houses that encouraged unsavory conduct" that could have their liquor licenses revoked and be closed down at will.

The Stonewall Inn, at 51 Christopher Street in Greenwich Village, first opened its doors during the Great Depression in 1930, converted from horse stables built in the 1700's. Over the decades it had been a banquet hall, had hosted wedding receptions and business functions, but by the 1960's it was a rundown dive, operated by organized crime. The Mob owned many gay bars in lower Manhattan, as they knew how to bribe corrupt officials. The owners of the Stonewall skirted the law and the need for a liquor license by operating it as a private club. A bouncer peered through a peephole in the front door and decided whether or not to admit patrons, just as a speakeasy operated in the 1930's. Carrying a warrant for the illegal sale of alcohol, eight police officers entered the Stonewall late on the night of Friday, June 17, 1969. Lights flashed, the music was turned off, and everyone stopped dancing.

The police ordered the two hundred or so patrons and several employees to line up and produce identification. Men who were cross-dressers (which was still illegal) and those without identification were arrested. A crowd started to gather in the street outside. When the police wagons arrived, the mood turned ugly. Catcalls and boos rang out. When some of those arrested resisted, struck defiant poses, or tried to escape, the taunting crowd threw cans, rocks, coins, or whatever was available at the officers. Some of the eight cops retreated to their van and called for riot police. The still-growing crowd stormed the door of the Stonewall and rammed it open with an uprooted parking meter. Policemen fought back, and then turned on a fire hose into the building.

A reporter for the *Village Voice* saw demonstrators being beaten. Helmeted riot police arrived with billy clubs and tear gas, and after two hours of rioting, the prisoners were taken to jail and the crowd was dispersed. No one was killed or seriously injured.

By next morning, graffiti appeared on the boarded up The

Stonewall Inn: "They Invaded Our Rights, Support Gay Power," and similar sentiments. Hundreds of protesters marched through Greenwich Village on that Saturday, June 18th night, chanting "Gay Power!" The Stonewall Inn reopened the same night, and again riot police clashed with protestors. For the first time, homosexuals engaged in public displays of affection as an act of defiance. On Sunday, activists tried to channel this new energy, some arguing that the violence was hurting the cause and others distributing flyers advocating that the momentum continue. The *Village Voice* came out on Wednesday June 22nd with the only front page coverage of the event, declaring "the liberation is underway." The third, final, and most violent riot occurred that night on 7th Avenue and Christopher Street. No other New York newspaper carried the story as a front page event. The *New York Post* buried it in back pages under the scornful headline, "Homo Nest Raided, Queen Bees Are Stinging Mad."

The *New York Post* headline story dripped with sarcasm and included every gay slur common in that era. Such was the treatment from the media at that time. Five other gay bars in the neighborhood had been raided or closed in the two weeks before the "Stonewall Uprising" and the Stonewall itself had been raided earlier the same week. The difference was, this time, gays fought back. They were fed up, and they channeled the same rebellious energy that was driving the civil rights and other movements into their own movement.

Inspired by their reaction, gay men, lesbians, bisexuals, transsexuals and transgendered people found a new strength in "coming out," and joining in. A new movement was born. The Gay Pride movement had a long path to travel, with many dangers and setbacks.

In March of 1970, less than a year later, the very same police officer who led the original Stonewall raid served papers for liquor and fire code violations at another Greenwich Village gay bar that was nearby called The Snake Pit. Police Deputy Inspector Seymour Pine brazenly (and illegally), arrested all of the one hundred and sixty patrons, bartenders and Snake Pit managers, and ordered them all to the nearby police station. He did so, he said later, to prevent another unruly crowd reaction. The prisoners were all given summonses for disorderly conduct that were later dismissed by the court. But those arrested did not know at the time that their charges were dismissed, since it was the middle of the night and many were disoriented or drunk. One gay man, an Argentinean named Diego Vinales, panicked because he was arrested with everyone else at The Snake Pit. He was in the country on a visa (which could have been revoked for homosexuality) and Vinales tried to escape from the precinct house. He jumped out of a second floor window, misjudged his jump and impaled himself on the fourteen-inch spike of a wrought-iron fence. Other men in the holding cells overheard police officers saying callously, "You don't have to hurry [with the ambulance], he's probably dead." Diego Vinales did live, and the new self-identified gay community again exploded in riots and protest marches.

Surprised by their militant reactions, the authorities slowly began to respond to the gay community as a political force. The administrations of Mayor John Lindsay and Governor Nelson Rockefeller reluctantly allowed changes to take place. As attitudes changed, lesbian women and gay men found bars and taverns that accepted them and the police raids finally ended.

Although Jimmy was not affiliated with any political activist groups, he followed the various gay pride events by reading about them in all the New York newspapers and by watching television news. He particularly liked reading about the gay movement in the *Village Voice*, which kept him informed and gave him something to speak about with his gay friends. Through all those historic years of change and public acceptance in Greenwich Village, Jimmy continued to visit the area, walk its streets, and frequent the various shops and gay bars.

Jimmy often went to a piano bar called The Monster at Grove Street and Sheridan Square in the West Village. The Monster is well known as a West Village institution. Jimmy used to walk in the bar at street level where the piano lounge was. Today, the decor hasn't changed much in 25 years. Patrons can pull up a stool and find a friendly crowd, some of which often sing along with the piano player. There is also a downstairs dance floor and a show room where patrons can find entertaining drag shows. Jimmy enjoyed watching the shows and dancing; but most of all, he liked watching the piano players so that he could observe their style on the keys and learn their musical techniques.

Even though Jimmy was the victim of muggers in the streets of New York and on the subway, he was not afraid and never felt uneasy in the City. Perhaps he felt that if he survived what happened to him in Vietnam, he could survive anything that a mugger could do. Because of his nervous breakdown, Jimmy was also naive and innocent. Nevertheless he showed no fear when he walked the streets of Greenwich Village.

Chapter 11 - Why Are You Yelling, Mike?

AS THE YEARS passed following his Navy discharge, Jimmy's life settled into a comfortable routine. He worked with his father and brothers in the stained glass studio during the week. In his spare time he did landscaping, cut grass, trimmed hedges, and picked up litter for the neighbors, which gave him extra spending money for his other life. He would escape on weekends from his humdrum existence in Charleston, to the wide open hedonism of Greenwich Village. Jimmy's over drinking and commuting late at night seemed to attract trouble, which resulted in him being an easy target for muggers. Even though he was repeatedly beaten up and mugged on the subway, the Staten Island Ferry, and on the streets of New York, he kept returning to Manhattan.

Jimmy liked going to nightclubs with live entertainment. He particularly liked listening to piano players and would sit for hours sipping beer and watching them play the keyboard. Jimmy also cruised other gay bars in search of needed companionship, in order to diminish his loneliness. One wet spring morning in April 1970, Mike, Sr., Mickey, and Jim Anderson were working on various stages of making stained glass windows on the benches of the glass studio.

Mickey said, "Where's Jimmy, Dad? I thought he was working today."

AI woke him an hour ago." Mike, Sr. growled, "I don't know what's taking him so long. He was probably drunk again."

"Want me to go check on him?" Mickey asked.

"No, I'll go myself. I'm fed up with him." Mike put his tools down in frustration. "He wakes me up every time he comes home late at night."

Mickey recognized his father's temper was about to blow. From long experience, he knew that it could rage one moment and be calm the next. Once Mike vented his anger, he usually calmed down, forgave, and was fine again. Jim Anderson wisely kept his mouth shut and stayed out of the way. Mike strode out the side door of the glass studio and went into the house. In the kitchen, Mary and Jimmy sat at the table. They had just finished breakfast.

Mike came in the side door. Mary greeted him cheerfully, but Mike was intent on having it out with his son. He reminded him that work began at eight and that on nights before workdays Jimmy shouldn't be carousing. Furthermore, his Greenwich Village friends did not pay his salary. Jimmy was predictably contrite.

Mike and Jimmy walked out the side door together and went into the stained glass studio to work. That incident was the start of a series when Jimmy did not show up for work on time, or he came home late at night and woke his father up.

Nevertheless, Jimmy was a hard worker and enjoyed being around his father and brothers in the studio making stained glass windows. He was eager to learn and asked the right questions about how to cut glass in fine shapes or how to solder the lead joints. Both Mike and Mickey gladly told him how to do and demonstrated the artistic techniques for him. Once he learned enough, Jimmy had it in mind to secretly make his own personal stained glass windows. Like learning the piano, there were many trials and errors when it came to cutting glass, but he slowly learned the trade.

While Jimmy's intentions were good, his yearning for his friends and the excitement of Greenwich Village kept drawing him to the City. He would sometimes go during the work week and get home very late, which in turn caused him to oversleep and not be at work on time. If there were windows to be set at a church, Mike and Mickey would want to leave the shop by 8:00 AM. If Jimmy was not there, they would become angry and leave without him. Jimmy would miss out on a day's pay and suffer the anger of his family. There were many times when personal conflict erupted between Jimmy and his father, especially when one or both men were in a bad mood. Sometimes the two men became so angry at each other that they came to physical blows. It was evident to any subjective observer that a major change was needed.

74

Chapter 12 - Move Out of This House!

ON A MILD Wednesday evening in March, 1985, Jimmy was on his way into the City. He stood on the deck of the Staten Island Ferry staring at the fog as it hung over the mouth of the Hudson River. The lights of the Manhattan shoreline glittered through the misty curtain, revealing the New York City skyline. Jimmy was dressed in his black leather pants, black cowboy boots and a black leather jacket, with a red shirt. He was on one of his forays to The Ramrod Club. Attending this club virtually guaranteed drinking too much, returning late, and oversleeping, which infuriated Michael, Sr. That night Jimmy came home around 2:30 AM, in a bad mood, which exacerbated the inevitable conflict between him and his father. The cooped-up anger and resentment between Jimmy and his father all came to a head.

Michael and Mary were comfortably sleeping in their twin beds. The front door slammed shut, which immediately woke Michael up from a sound sleep. Michael was a light sleeper and would wake-up at the drop of a pin.

Michael heard sounds of dishes in the kitchen. He looked at the alarm clock. His blood pressure started to rise as he got out of bed, put on his bathrobe and slippers, and walked into the hall. He looked downstairs. Both the hall and kitchen lights were on. Mike could hear Jimmy clumsily rummaging in the refrigerator. Something dropped to the floor and shattered.

"Jimmy, what the hell are you doing down there," Mike shouted?

Jimmy shouted back, "I'm getting something to eat. I dropped a glass."

The men's loud voices awakened Mary. She sat up in bed and asked, "What are you yelling about, Mike?"

Mike yelled from the hall, "Your Goddamn drunken son woke me up again."

"He's your son too," Mary replied.

Michael rumbled downstairs and into the kitchen. Jimmy sat at the table with a glass of orange juice and a ham and cheese sandwich. An argument quickly ensued, with Mike trying to lay down the law and Jimmy arguing that he paid rent and could come and go as he wanted. When he criticized Mike for yelling at his wife, Mike's emotional thermostat went haywire.

Jimmy said, "I can't help it if my friends live in the City."

Mike growled, "You waste your time with your queer friends."

"That's because I'm a queer, too. You get it?" Jimmy challenged with his eyes blazing.

Mike moved close to Jimmy and yelled in his face. "I want you to move the hell out of my house. You get it? I've had enough of your shit."

Jimmy pushed him away, yelling, "Get out of my face, you dam' grouch. I've had enough of your screaming and yelling!"

Mary entered the room, clearly upset that her husband and son were fighting. She moved to stand between them. Grasping at the arms of the two taller men, she said, "Calm down Mike. Sit down, Jimmy."

Mike was still staring at Jimmy. He said, "Dammit, I won't calm down. This bullshit has gone on long enough."

He pounded his fist down on the table, and knocked the glass of orange juice onto the floor. Jimmy grabbed Mike by the lapels of his robe.

Jimmy yelled, "Look what you did to my drink, asshole."

With that insult, Mike had enough and his temper got the best of him. He punched Jimmy hard in the face. Jimmy was knocked backwards from the blow, but recovered. Angry, he counter punched, hitting Mike on the chin with a partial uppercut.

Upset and not wanting her husband and son to fight, Mary pushed between them. She cried out, "Stop it! The two of you – just, stop!"

Blinded and deafened by their mutual anger, Mike and Jimmy ignored Mary. The two men closed on each other again swinging, but they both accidently bumped into Mary. She was knocked down to the floor. Stunned by what they had done, they both stopped fighting and helped her get to a chair. Mary was crying. Jimmy handed her a tissue.

Mike said, "I didn't mean to knock you over, honey. I'm sorry."

Jimmy said sadly, "Sorry Mom. It was an accident. I'd never hurt you."

Mary said, sobbing, "Why must the two of you always fight? Jimmy, you're like a lamb when you're sober and a lion when you drink."

Mike said loudly, "Your son has no respect for us, or my wishes. I want him to move... the hell... out of this house!"

Mary dabbed her eyes with a tissue and said, "Be reasonable, Mike. Where would he go?"

"That's his problem. He's 38 years old! Jimmy, I want you out by the weekend. That's final." Mike stormed out of the kitchen and went back up the stairs to his bedroom.

Jimmy held his Mother's hand and said to her, "I'm sick and tired of him treating me like a child. I work hard around here."

Mary said, "I know you do, Jimmy. But you heard your Father."

"I'll move out then. I'll figure something out," Jimmy said, turning away.

Mary twisted a tissue in her hand and said, "You could ask your brother Bobby if he has room for you. He just rented a house in Clay

Pit Pond State Park, not that far."

"That's a good idea, Mom," Jimmy said, patting her arm. "I'll see him tomorrow. Let me help you upstairs, Mom, so you can go back to bed."

Chapter 13 - Basement...I Could Sleep There

AFTER ROBERT'S DIVORCE from his first wife, Letty in 1975, he rented a two bedroom apartment off Richmond Avenue in the Travis section of Staten Island. Within two months, Leticia asked him to take their three youngest children, realizing she was not able to give them the discipline and care they needed due to her drinking problem. Robert accepted her offer and gladly took his children, but did not realize what a monumental task this would be, but somehow managed to hold down his job and raise his four children. He was fortunate and was able to get assistance from New York City Child Services, who provided a nanny to watch the children after school and prepare meals.

In 1984, when Robert rented a small house from New York State on the property of Clay Pit Pond State Park, his oldest daughter, Debbie, also moved in with him. Robert was still working at the Staten Island Zoo but was promoted by the new Zoo Director, George Zappler, to Assistant Curator of Herpetology and Education. This position not only allowed him to give lectures and classes to school groups, but he was also able to do field studies and research on reptiles and amphibians. In the spring of 1972, Robert was awarded a research grant from the National Audubon Society to begin studies on the bog turtle (Glyptemys [Clemmys] muhlenbergii), a small marsh turtle from eastern United States that was listed as "endangered" in most states where it occurred. Bob's work with this endangered species inspired the founding of his environmental consulting company, Herpetological Associates, Inc. in 1977 and to take charge of his life more fully.

One sunny afternoon in March, 1985, Bobby sat at his desk writing a report. There was a knock on the front door. It was Jimmy.

Robert said, "Hi Jimmy, come in. What's up?"

In subdued tones, Jimmy related that their mother had suggested he speak with Robert about staying with him. A few questions were all Robert needed to understand that the long-time antagonism between father and son had reached a point of no return. Jimmy had until the weekend to find a new place to live.

Robert answered, "I'm in this small house with all my kids. I don't have an extra bedroom for you."

"I could pay you room and board," Jimmy pleaded. "The same as I paid Mom and Dad."

"That's not the issue Jimmy. It's space." Robert said, "Look around. Every inch of space is filled. The only place no one is sleeping is in the basement."

"The basement! Hey, I could sleep down there," Jimmy suggested.

"You wouldn't mind that?" Robert asked with wonder.

"No. I don't have any other choice right now."

The brothers clumped down the cellar stairs. The bare cement-block-walled room was partially lit by four small windows, two on each side of the foundation. A washing machine and dryer were to the left of the entrance. Boxes and fish tanks were stored along one wall. Robert tugged a string to a bare light bulb on the ceiling, and the light illuminated the basement with a stark glare.

"There's plenty of room down here. I could clean it up." Jimmy pointed, "Put my bed there."

"Well, if you don't mind being in the cellar," Robert said doubtfully. With more warmth he added, "You're welcome to stay here, Jimmy."

Jimmy said with enthusiasm, "I could move this stuff to the other side. Put my rug down. Would you mind if I paint?"

Robert laughed. "Do anything you want to make the place livable. The only thing I ask is don't bring your gay friends overnight. I don't want the kids to be confused. I'll tell them you're moving in with us when they get home from school."

"Don't worry Bobby," Jimmy said. "I love your kids."

Robert gave his brother a ride to pick up his belongings, and on the way let Jimmy know he did not have to pay rent. Buying his own food and helping Robert keep the place clean was enough.

Jimmy grinned. "You're a good brother. It's a deal."

Brother Bobby had his four children with him in the house: Debbie, Kelly, Robert Jr. and Michael. Robert's older daughter, Debbie had just recently come to live with her father. Jimmy fixed comfortable living quarters in the basement of the overcrowded house. He kept his word and never brought any of his male companions to the house to stay overnight. However, he continued his weekend trips into the City to visit his friends and carouse at the gay bars. During the week, he made extra money by doing gardening and yard work for neighbors in Charleston.

Because he was still angry with his father, Jimmy avoided him by visiting his mother when Mike was away working. When Jimmy went into the City, he would ask his brother to drive him to the Rapid Transit train station in Pleasant Plains.

Bobby and his children enjoyed having Jimmy living with them. It gave the brothers a chance to re-connect and get to know each other as adults. It was during one of these long private conversations that Jimmy revealed to his brother what happened to him in Vietnam, how his friend had been murdered and he was almost killed. Dredging up the memories rattled Jimmy. He began to cry passionately. In an effort to comfort his brother, Robert told him that both good things and bad things happen for a reason, even if people cannot understand why these things happen.

"We have to learn to 'roll with the punches that God hits us with,' accept the good along with the bad, and try to learn from it all. No matter how bad things get, just keep on living your life and treat others the way you want to be treated."

"You sound like Mommy," Jimmy sniffed. "She always tells me that."

"I guess that's where I heard it. She told me the same thing."

Jimmy helped Bob by watching the kids for him while he was away doing field work on endangered reptiles and amphibians. He cooked simple meals like grilled cheese sandwiches, hamburgers and French fries, or else heated TV dinners in the oven. He also helped by keeping the house clean, and doing yard work, planting flowers, mowing the lawn, and generally adding visual beauty to his life and those of ones he loved around him.

The wood frame house on Carlin Street was small, but the rent was affordable for Robert, whose days were challenged in building his environmental consulting business, Herpetological Associates, Inc., and keeping a nice home for his children. Everything about the house was small. The rooms, windows, even the doorways were of tiny proportions. The door openings measured just 6'2" from floor to moldings, which was alright for anyone under six feet in height. However, these short door jams turned out to be not so good for Mike, Jr. (who stood 6'3"), the first time he came to visit Bobby and Jimmy at their Carlin Street home. On June 30, 1985, Mary asked Mickey to bring Jimmy mail and his pension check. Mary called first to make sure they were home and let them know Mickey would arrive soon. A half hour later there was a knock on the front door. Bobby got up from his desk, walked out to the front porch and opened the door.

"Oh, hi, Mickey. Come on in," Bobby invited. He extended his right hand to his brother.

"Hi Bobby. Where's Jimmy?"

"He's in his room in the basement, reading. Come on in. We were just going to have lunch, why don't you join us?"

"Okay, that sounds good. What do you have," Mickey asked?

"Ham, cheese, turkey and rye bread. Everything you like. Just watch out for the low doorways."

As Bobby spoke his last words, his taller brother slammed his forehead into the top wood molding of the kitchen doorway.

"Son of a bitch! These doorways are low," Mickey exclaimed.

"Sorry, I tried to tell you to duck." Bobby said apologetically.

Jimmy emerged from the basement greeted his big brother, and received his mail.

Along with a sandwich, Mike had hot Lipton tea with milk and sugar. Jimmy drank his favorite: chilled orange juice. Over the next half hour, the three Zappalorti boys sat at the kitchen table having their lunch and enjoyed each other's conversation about their work and lives.

Mickey took a last sip of tea. He stood and asked, "Where's the bathroom?"

Bobby pointed to the door at the end of the kitchen.

The lesson Mickey had learned walking into the kitchen was forgotten. He struck his head on the opposite wooden door frame with a resounding whack.

"Holy Shit! Who the fuck lived here, midgets?" yelled Mickey as he grabbed his head.

Bobby and Jimmy looked at each other and chuckled as they cleared off the table and moved it flush with the kitchen's side wall. The sound of Mickey opening the bathroom door filtered into the kitchen, directly followed by a loud thump and a louder yell.

"Son of a bitch!" Mickey yelled his oft-used exclamation. He rubbed his forehead again.

Jimmy laughed. "The first two hits must have given you amnesia."

Bobby tried to restrain from smiling, but he laughed too.

Mickey muttered. "It's not funny. My head hurts like hell." As he came through the kitchen, he walked right into the chandelier, because Bobby and Jimmy had pushed the table back to the wall. He hit his head on the light as it swung back and forth. Mike yelled, "What kind of house is this?"

Bobby and Jimmy were trying to withhold their laughter as Mike quickly walked towards the door out of the kitchen. He did not duck and struck his forehead on the low doorway again.

Mike yelled, "I'm getting the fuck out of here before I kill myself."

He escaped through the front door while rubbing his head. Bobby and Jimmy slapped at their knees and laughed until tears rolled down their cheeks. Mickey never returned to that small house on Carlin Street.

In order to save his money for his long-awaited trip to Italy, Jimmy continued doing part time gardening work in Charleston and, when he could, saving something from his Navy pension checks. Not having to pay Bobby rent helped. In March of 1986, a much larger four bedroom house on Sharrotts Road became available from Clay Pit Pond Sate Park, and Bobby rented it. The additional room allowed each daughter to have her own bedroom. By then, Jimmy had made up with his father and moved back to live with his parents on Androvette Street.

Chapter 14 - Two Cities, Two Jimmys

JIMMY'S COMMUTE ON public transportation involved a ride on the Rapid Transit train from Princes Bay to the Staten Island Ferry Terminal. From there, he would take the Staten Island Ferry across New York Harbor and the mouth of the Hudson River, to the Battery in lower Manhattan. He liked to sit on the top deck, especially in the summer. On June 21, 1985, the ferry was moving at full steam toward lower Manhattan. On the north side of the boat, the Statue of Liberty was in clear view to all its passengers. On the upper deck, several tourists were taking pictures. A young Latino couple with their arms around each other stared in amazement. Jimmy stood alongside them. He often positioned himself near the bow of the ferry boat, because it reminded him of his Navy years and his friend, Tom when he served aboard the USS Henrico.

Standing on the upper deck also gave him a good view of the Manhattan sky-line and the gleaming Twin Towers which loomed over southern Manhattan. If Jimmy could have driven a car, he would surely have reached Manhattan over the Verrazano Narrows Bridge that connected Staten Island to Brooklyn and then taken the Belt Parkway to the Battery Tunnel or the Brooklyn-Queens Expressway to the Brooklyn Bridge. But that was not the case. Both Michael, Sr. and Mary tried to teach Jimmy how to drive, but he was too nervous, too uncoordinated and unable to concentrate on controlling a moving motor vehicle. Once when Mary was instructing him, he failed to look both ways and almost had a serious accident with a bus on Arthur Kill Road. After that, everyone agreed it was too risky for him to attempt to drive. So instead, Jimmy had to use public transportation.

Jimmy often fled from quiet, conservative Staten Island to the bright lights and night life of New York City. Like a caterpillar that changes from a chrysalis to a butterfly, when Jimmy crossed over into Manhattan, he metamorphosed. He felt free and uninhibited. It seemed as if he was a different person. Two cities, two Jimmys.

On that June day, Jimmy had dressed in black slacks and a blue shirt. He also had a black leather vest over the shirt, black belt and cowboy boots, all of which matched his vest. He held a copy of the Village Voice newspaper in his hand. Jimmy was crossing over into his "other world" for a specific reason. He had been learning to play the piano for five years. He could not read music, so he depended on his mother, Mary, Jim Anderson and his brother, Robert to show him some basic chords and melodies. Jim Anderson and his brother, Robert played in a top forty band, called The Careless Five, for fifteen years together, so they knew music.

Jimmy used to go to listen to his brother's music. Like his brother, Jimmy wanted to entertain in clubs and have people dance to his music. He was determined to play the songs that he loved. While learning, he nearly drove his parents crazy by playing the same songs over and over, ad nauseam. Through trial-and-error and endless practicing, he finally was satisfied with the way he could play. His mission on that warm day was to audition at a night club and get hired to entertain people.

Jimmy took a pack of Marlboro cigarettes from his shirt pocket and lit one. He turned from the railing, walked to a wooden bench, and sat. He opened the Village Voice newspaper and found the Want Ad section for musicians. He thumbed through the columns looking for piano players. Carefully perusing the page, he finally found one that read: Part time piano player wanted for weekends. Must audition! Ask for Marty Coppersmith at the Pink Flamingo bar in the Village.

Jimmy circled the ad, wrote down the phone number, and then looked up at the Twin Towers in lower Manhattan and smiled. Jimmy felt the rumble of the ferry's engines. The captain had reversed its engines to slow it down as it neared the dock. As soon as he reached a bay of public phones, Jimmy dialed the number of The Pink Flamingo. He spoke with the manager, who told him to come for his audition at 3:30 P.M. Jimmy made his connection from the ferry to the subway train which took him uptown to Greenwich Village. He was sitting in the center of the subway car looking at the people around him.

The uneven tracks caused the car to rock back and forth. Also in the car was a sleazy-looking man with a narrow face and flat nose with long hair growing from his nostrils. He badly needed a shave. He was dressed in brown slacks and a wrinkled brown suit jacket and stood several seats from Jimmy. Across from him, wearing leather and chains, was a young punk rocker guy his girlfriend, smoking a joint and giggling. They offered a drag to Jimmy, but he smiled and shook his head. He wanted to have a clear mind for his audition. Sitting a few seats up from Jimmy were two Puerto Rican woman wearing summer flower dresses and carrying shopping bags. They looked at the young punk rocker guy and his girlfriend with patent disapproval. Several others sat with their backs to Jimmy. Standing near the front of the subway car was a business man in a neatly pressed gray suit, white shirt and red tie reading a newspaper.

The sleazy character slowly moved toward the man. The subway car slowed and then lurched forward again, causing the sleazy guy to bump into the business man. The sleazy man had used the moment to reach into the business man's back pocket and steal his wallet. The thief swiftly slipped the wallet into his suit jacket pocket. Jimmy, who was usually observant about his surroundings, saw what happened. He jumped out of his seat, ran to the end of the car, and approached the sleazy guy.

"Hey you, I saw that!" Jimmy exclaimed.

The sleazy guy's head reared back. "What the fuck are you talking about?"

Jimmy said, "I saw you take his wallet!"

The sleazy guy replied, "You didn't see shit. What wallet?"

Before the thief knew what had happened, Jimmy reached into his pocket like a magic trick and pulled out the wallet. He held it up for the business man to see.

"This wallet!" Jimmy yelled.

The sleazy guy tried to grab the wallet back, but Jimmy moved away from him and towards the man. Everyone in the train car was now watching the altercation. The thief grabbed at Jimmy, pulling at his hands, but Jimmy pushed him away.

"Give me my fucking wallet, or I'll belt you in the mouth!" the sleazy guy threatened.

Instead, Jimmy handed the wallet to the businessman in the gray suit. The man looked at it, opened it, and recognized it as his own. He stood-up with indignity.

"Back off and leave this man alone, or I'll call the Transit Police when we get to the next station!"

Not wanting to get arrested, the sleazy guy retreated to the opposite end of the subway car and went through the door into the next car. The business man sat down and Jimmy sat next to him.

"Thank you for getting my wallet back. That was a brave thing you did."

"You're welcome," Jimmy replied. AI know what it's like to lose your wallet. I've been robbed a few times."

"Well, if I can ever do anything to repay you for your kindness, please give me a call. Here's my card."

The business man handed Jimmy his business card. Jimmy examined at it and then placed it in his wallet. The train came into the Christopher Street station and stopped. The sleazy guy ran out the door and intermingled with the people on the subway platform.

"This is my stop," Jimmy said smiling as he shook the man's

hand. "Goodbye."

"Goodbye, Jimmy. Thanks again."

Jimmy quickly walked out the door as it closed behind him. The man waved through the glass windows on the door. Jimmy walked up the stairs and onto Christopher Street. He checked the address of The Pink Flamingo and walked towards his destination.

The Pink Flamingo bar was a nicely decorated night club with wall to wall mirrors separated by wide painted panels of tropical palm trees and flamingo birds standing in water. The tables were covered with blue tablecloths with pink borders. Blue and pink neon lights bordered the mirrors. The reflection of the neon lights cast a colorful mood in the bar. On a raised stage at the end of the bar sat an ebony baby grand piano. A large dance floor was opposite the stage.

A few patrons sat at the bar drinking and chatting a couple speaking with Bernie, the bartender. Jimmy sat at the bar as well, sipping a glass of Coke. An elderly man was at the piano, playing a classic song. He finished his piece and looked at the club owner, Marty Coppersmith.

"Okay, Paul," Marty said. AThat gives me an idea of your style of playing. I'll let you know what I decide. I have one more audition today. Thanks." The man got up from the stool and exited the bar. Marty Coppersmith turned and looked at Jimmy.

"Okay, Jimmy... Let's see what you got. Play me some tunes" Marty said.

Jimmy sat at the piano. He suddenly had an attack of stage fright. He took a drag of his cigarette and looked for an ashtray. Bernie walked over and gave him one. Then Jimmy took a sip of his drink and looked for a coaster. Immediately, Bernie put a coaster on the piano and Jimmy placed his glass on it. Jimmy looked at Bernie, then at the club owner, Marty and smiled. He adjusted his distance from the piano keys and his feet to the foot pedals. Then he started to play the song made popular by Tony Bennett, "I Left My Heart in San

Francisco." As he played his music, some of the patrons stopped chatting looked up. Soon, a few more people entered the bar and watched the guy at the piano keys. Some of them came up to the piano.

The club owner, Marty smiled and looked at Bernie the bartender. Bernie smiled back and gave him a "thumbs-up." After completing his first song, without hesitation Jimmy went right into another, made famous by Frank Sinatra, "I've got you under my skin."

The club owner tapped the table with his pen and swayed to the rhythm of the song. As Jimmy continued to play, just the way he had rehearsed it over and over again, his confidence grew. Everyone in the room was watching and listening. Jimmy liked the way it made him feel. He felt a sense of importance, something he had not felt since he had joined the Navy years ago. He was being acknowledged, respected, and was the center of attention.

The owner of The Pink Flamingo, hired Jimmy on the spot and offered him $30.00 a night, plus free drinks. Marty Coppersmith didn't know it, but Jimmy probably would have played in his club for free. All those hours, days and years of practicing his music finally paid-off. Jimmy was very happy, because he could now entertain people with his musical talent and get paid for it. Life was good!

Jimmy returned Friday and Saturday nights as the official piano player at The Pink Flamingo bar. The regular patrons took a liking to him and his music. He soon had a crowd of people coming to hear him play and to dance to his music every weekend. Jimmy became friends with Marty and Bernie, along with many of the regular neighborhood patrons. The more he played the piano, the better he got at it. Jimmy felt appreciated, wanted, and at home at The Pink Flamingo.

Jimmy returned to The Pink Flamingo on the July 4, 1985,

weekend. The bar was crowded, smoke filled, and nicely decorated in red, white, and blue for the July Fourth holiday. There were balloons taped to the mirrors, and the pink and blue neon lights reflected light off them. Dozens of people were drinking at the bar. Gay and lesbian couples danced Jimmy's rendition of the Fats Domino song, "Blueberry Hill." Everyone was having a fun time. Lou Epstein, a flamboyant 31 year old gay man, sipped his drink at the bar. Lou was Jewish, stood five feet eight inches tall, and weighed 136 pounds. He had brown eyes, brown hair, and a thin mustache.

"Hey, Bernie," Lou Epstein said. "Who's the guy playing piano?"

"His name is Jimmy," Bernie said. "He's been playing piano here about a month."

"He sure is cute," Lou said. "Where's he from?"

Bernie replied, "Staten Island."

"He has his own style, but it's good," Lou judged.

"Yeah, he is good," Bernie said. "Marty told him he would make lots of tips. So, if you like his music, throw him something."

"Yeah, I think I will," Lou said.

Lou took two dollar bills from his pocket and gracefully strutted to the piano. He winked at Jimmy and put the money in the tip glass. Then he gave Jimmy a big smile.

"Hey thanks, I appreciate that," Jimmy said while smiling back.

"You're welcome," Lou said. "Can you play 'Run Around Sue'?"

"Sure, I know it, Jimmy replied. "I'll play it for you next."

"I'll listen from the bar," Lou said. "By the way, I'm Lou...'Run Around Lou.'"

Jimmy laughed and said, "Hi Lou...I'm Jimmy."

At closing time, Jimmy promised to be back next Friday and Saturday. The audience applauded, Jimmy stood, smiled, and took a bow. Then he grabbed his tips from the glass. He walked over to where Lou was sitting at the bar.

"I enjoyed your playing, Jim. How long have you been at it," Lou asked?

"About seven years," Jimmy answered.

Lou said, "Can I buy you a drink?

"Sure, I could go for a nightcap. I'll have another Budweiser!"

Lou gestured for a beer, which Bernie immediately brought over and placed it front of Jimmy.

"So Jimmy, Bernie told me you're from Staten Island," Lou said. "That's a long trip to make this late at night."

"It sure is, especially when I'm tired and had too much to drink," Jimmy confessed.

"Well, listen, my roommate is away for the weekend," Lou informed. "You're more than welcome to stay at our place tonight."

Jimmy considered the invitation and then said, "Okay. I'll take you up on your offer. I'm really tired."

"It's settled then. You'll come home with me," Lou said while smiling.

It was through this chance meeting at The Pink Flamingo with Lou Epstein that Jimmy would soon meet Epstein's roommate, Don Shepler, who would become his life-long best friend and companion. Lou initially thought Jimmy had high potential as his boyfriend, but, he was wrong. Lou was in for a surprise and had no idea what Jimmy really wanted. Lou had never met anyone quite like Jimmy before.

Lou and Jimmy entered the apartment Lou's apartment in Greenwich Village. It was large and nicely decorated with numerous expensive pictures and antique furniture. Hanging over the dining room table was a crystal chandelier that immediately caught Jimmy's eye.

"Beautiful," Jimmy declared. "I love crystal. I purchased one for my parents last Christmas, but not as nice as this."

"It's Don's. He specializes in antiques and decorating," Lou said. "Most of the furniture in here is his."

"You guys really have a nice place," said Jimmy. "I'd like to have an apartment like this someday."

"I'll show you around the apartment," Lou said. He guided Jimmy into the living room, which was filled with marvelous antique furniture. The top of the dresser had various pictures of Lou, Don, Don's parents and other friends. Jimmy studied all the pictures.

"This must be Don," Jimmy surmised. "Nice looking man. Are you guys a couple?"

"We were for a while, but now we're just friends," Lou answered. "We have an understanding. We see other people when the opportunity presents itself. We share the apartment for financial reasons. You want a nightcap?"

"Another beer would be great," Jimmy said.

"San Miguel?" Lou offered.

"What's that?" asked Jimmy

"It's a brand of beer," Lou responded.

"If you say so, but do have any Bud?" Jimmy asked.

Lou just laughed. Jimmy turned and continued to stare at the crystal chandelier. He went into the kitchen and opened the refrigerator. "You really like that, huh?"

"I love it," Jimmy replied.

"Well, it's okay if you like gaudy things," Lou said as he reentered the room with the beers. "Have a seat on the couch."

Lou opened the beers, filled the glasses and handed one to Jimmy. Jimmy took the glass and sat down on the couch, but he's still staring at the chandelier. "Thanks, Lou. I'm very thirsty," Jimmy said. Jimmy sipped his beer and smacked his lips, then looked up at Lou. Lou went over to a stereo and put on some soft music. Then he walked to a dimmer switch and lowered the lighting in the room. He walked back and sat next to Jimmy on the couch.

"Wow, that sure made a difference," Jimmy said.

"Of course it did," Lou replied. "That was my plan."

"Yeah, it made the chandelier change colors," Jimmy said. "I can't take my eyes off it."

The chandelier proved a rival that Lou was having trouble besting. Finally, he said, ALook Jimmy, why don't we go to bed and have a little fun?"

Jimmy finally took his eyes off the crystal chandelier. He looked at Lou carefully.

"What do you mean?" Jimmy asked

"I mean, that's Don's room over there," replied Lou while pointing. "And mine...mine's right there. What's your choice?"

"I think I just want to go to sleep, if that's okay," Jimmy said.

"You're one in a million, Jimmy," Lou sighed, shaking his head. He rose from the couch, looked down at Jimmy, who was still staring at the chandelier, and headed toward his bedroom.

"No matter how long you stare at it, the channel won't change," Lou said sarcastically.

Jimmy flashed him another smile.

Disappointed, but too drunk and tired to argue, Lou answered, "Can't blame a guy for trying. Good night, Jim." Lou retreated to his room. Jimmy settled back on the couch with his beer and continued to stare at the array of light reflecting off the crystals. After finishing another beer, Jimmy went to sleep right on the couch.

In the morning bright sunbeams streamed through the window, hitting the chandelier and reflecting onto Jimmy's face. Jimmy opened his eyes. The natural sunlight made the crystals gleam even more than the artificial light had the night before. Jimmy stood up and walked over to the edge of the dining room table to have a closer look at the crystal chandelier. Immediately, Jimmy noticed that it was covered with dust, which he did not like. Jimmy went into the kitchen and looked under the sink for cleaning products. He found some Windex spray, but when he picked it up he noticed a bottle of ammonia right behind it. His father had taught Jimmy a long time ago that ammonia and hot water was the best solution to clean glass. Jimmy found a pail and some paper towels. Piece by piece he washed each crystal, making sure all the dust was off. He removed the smaller pieces of crystal from their hooks and washed them in the bucket. Then he carefully dried and returned them to their hooks. As he stood on the step ladder he heard someone at the front door.

Lou's flat mate, Don Shepler, stood in the hall of the apartment building. He was clean-shaven, well-groomed hairdresser and antique collector. Originally from Connecticut, Don had moved to Manhattan at twenty-three to work in a hair salon.

However, his main interest was in antiques, especially fine furniture, chandeliers, and rugs. He became a part-time interior decorator with a large furniture store in the Village. He did so well that he stopped cutting hair and worked full time as an interior decorator. Don was fumbling with his keys at the front door. He had a newspaper and a coffee in his hands. Don turned the lock and pushed the door open. He stopped in his tracks

"Are you the new maid?" Don asked.

"Jimmy introduced himself from a small stepladder. He related that Lou had invited him to spend the night.

"Did he?" Don said. "He's smarter than I thought."

At that moment, Lou entered the room from the kitchen with a tray of breakfast food,

"Don! Meet Jimmy."

"Hard not to," Don said through a big smile.

Lou asked, "Jimmy, did you kill all of the San Miguel, last night?"

"Sorry. I'll replace it," Jimmy answered. "Could I give you beer instead?"

Don and Lou laughed at what they thought was a joke. Lou set the breakfast of orange juice, coffee, toast and jelly down on the table.

Jimmy came down from the ladder, looked up at the chandelier with satisfaction, and asked, "Doesn't she sparkle?"

"She sure does," Don said, admiring Jimmy's posterior.

Chapter 15 - Oh Yeah? Who's 'We'?

JIMMY WALKED FROM Don and Lou's apartment along Christopher Street. He stopped at a diner and purchased a cup of tea and a New York Daily News. Then he went down to the subway station and found an empty bench on the platform. He sipped his tea and noticed a New York Rapid Transit cop walking through the train station on his rounds. Satisfied nothing was wrong, the cop then went up the stairs. Jimmy sat on a bench waiting for the train to take him down to the Staten Island Ferry. He took another sip of his hot tea and continued to read the newspaper. He did not notice the three black men watching him from the other end of the platform. As soon as the cop was out of sight the thugs began walking toward Jimmy. The ring leader was about twenty-three year old, a tall man dressed in jeans, red tee-shirt, and sneakers. He was flanked by two confederates.

The leader instructed one associate to get on Jimmy's other side, then wait until the escape routes were blocked. The three gang members separated and got in position for the mugging. The subway station platform was quiet. Jimmy read his newspaper and did not notice the second thug as he moved toward him. The sound of the northbound train got louder as it pulled into station. The third walked slowly along the wall. The leader walked up the center of the platform.

The northbound train pulled away, revealing two elderly men as they walked towards the stairs. A young couple stopped to hug and kiss affectionately. Jimmy looked up, watched them kiss. As the young couple walked up the stairs and out of sight, the leader signaled to his buddies to move in.

"Hey, white boy," he called, "Gimme your wallet and watch!"

Jimmy, surprised and not aware of the other two men, said, "My friend, I'm not giving you anything! Get lost!"

"I said, gimme your fuckin' wallet, or we goin' to kick your ass."

Jimmy stood up, faced the man in defiance and said, "Oh yeah? Who's 'we'?"

From behind Jimmy, the second gang member said, "We be 'we', motherfucker!"

The third added, "Your wallet and jewelry, now!"

Jimmy turned around and saw the other two gang members behind him for the first time.

"Three of you," Jimmy said cautiously.

Jimmy made a dash for the exit stairs but was grabbed by two as he passed them. They punched him in the face and stomach. Jimmy tried to defend himself by punching the leader in the face, forcing him back. Then he turned toward the third one and hit him with two left jabs on the nose. Then Jimmy kicked the leader in the stomach which caused him to double over with his nose bleeding. Jimmy tried to catch his breath as the second pulled out a .38 special revolver, held it to Jimmy's head, and said, "I got one bullet just for you, motherfucker!"

The harshly spoken words triggered a mental flashback. Jimmy transported back instantly to the alley of Da Nang, the night he had almost died. He saw himself lying on the filthy ground in the alley. He saw his attacker as Pham Son-Tien, pointing a gun at his head.

The Vietnamese gangster Pham had said, "Last bullet just for you, queer boy!"

Jimmy screamed, "You beat Tom, you bastards. You cut Tom!" He yelled so loud, that it caught the other two gang members completely off guard.

Jimmy knocked the pistol out of his attacker's hand with a karate chop. He then kicked him in the balls and started running. The black men were quicker. One pistol whipped Jimmy in the face while another jumped on Jimmy and proceeded to beat him without mercy. They hauled Jimmy up against a wall, punched and beat him until he fell to the ground bleeding profusely.

At that moment, the New York City Transit cop came down the stairs carrying a cup of coffee. He saw what was happening, called for back-up, and blew his whistle. The three gangsters ran off in the opposite direction. The cop went to Jimmy, saw that he was bleeding badly and said, "Hold on, I'm going to get you help. What's your name?"

"Seaman Zappalorti, Sir," Jimmy said in a daze. "Seaman James Zappalorti, Sir." Still in flashback, he thought the cop was his buddy, Tom. Jimmy shouted, "You're here, Tom! I saw Pham beat you in the hotel room! How'd you get here?" The transit cop said, "You're in shock, kid. Just hold on. I've got to go upstairs after those punks. Just lie here. I'll be right back."

The cop ran in the same direction as the three gangsters. Jimmy struggled to his feet as the southbound train to the Battery came roaring into the station. The doors opened, and Jimmy staggered into a subway car. The train had several people in it. They stared in shock at Jimmy's bleeding nose and the cuts on his face from all the kicks and punches he received.

Jimmy returned their stares with a half smile.

"Got to get back to my ship. Don't want to be AWOL. No, no, no! Tom won't want to be AWOL. Tom, where are you?"

Jimmy collapsed onto a seat as the train pulled from the platform. He closed his eyes and started to cry. No one approached him to offer help. Finally, another New York City Transit cop entered the car from a connecting door. He was actively searching for Jimmy. Jimmy gave the cop his name and address, along with a statement about the attempted robbery and savage beating he had received at the Christopher Street station. The cop offered to take Jimmy to the hospital for a check-up, but he refused and said, "I just want to go home."

The subway train took Jimmy down to the Battery, where he made his connection to the Staten Island Ferry. An hour and a half later, he stepped-off the 113 bus on the corner of Androvette. He walked painfully down the street to his parents' house. Even though he had washed the blood off his face in the bathroom at the ferry terminal, his face was badly cut and bruised. At least the bleeding had stopped. He slowly walked down the street towards his house.

As Jimmy reached the corner a neighbor Mr. Owen Reiter, who was hosing his garden yelled, "Hey, Jimmy! Are you alright? What happened to you? You're all bloody, do you need help?

"No Owen, I'm okay. I was mugged and robbed on the subway this morning," Jimmy replied. "But I'll still cut your lawn and do a great job for you, Owen."

Although he was cut, bruised, in pain, and tired, he still wanted to help his neighbor. Jimmy leaned against the tree, closed his eyes, gathered what strength he had and then proceeded to his home.

The Christopher Street incident was just one of many, when Jimmy fell victim to robbers while traveling to and from New York City. Because he was always alone on the New York public transportation system and often traveled late at night, he was an easy target for muggers and thieves, especially when he had too much to drink. He was not afraid of the thieves because to his way of thinking if he had survived the experience in Vietnam, he could survive the mean streets of New York. Jimmy felt he could defend himself well enough to thwart any street punks, since robbery was their only motive. Jimmy's motive to play his music in Greenwich Village and see his friends was stronger. And, after all, he had survived so much that God must surely be protecting him.

Chapter 16 - I'm Part of That Statistic

THE FOLLOWING MONDAY, Michael, Mickey, Jim Anderson and Jimmy were working on various stages of creating stained glass windows in the studio. Each man had a specific job to do as they assembled the stained glass windows. The men assembled the windows diligently from various wooden shop benches. Using the pre-drawn cartoons as models, Mickey carefully hand painted individual pieces of colored glass. Jim Anderson soldered together the lead joints of another window. Mike, Sr. placed a paper template on a piece of blue glass and shaped it with a glass cutter. Jimmy carefully pushed putty under every piece of shaped lead on another new stained glass window. After a companionable silence, Mike Sr. asked, "So Jimmy, did you get to play piano at the club in the city Saturday night?"

Jimmy answered, "Yeah Dad, I played five sets and made my salary of twenty-five dollars and sixteen dollars in tips. The manager likes my music and invited me to play for another month on Friday and Saturday nights."

Jimmy looked at Jim Anderson and continued, "I'm glad you and Bobby taught me how to play the piano."

Jim Anderson said, "Hey, I just showed you a few songs, some basic chord progressions and some melodies. You did the rest by practicing."

"Yeah, he just about drove me and Mary crazy playing the same notes over and over," Mike teased. "Glad you taught him some new songs, Jim."

"It's good you found a place to play piano Jimmy, but be careful when you're coming home at night," added Mickey. "I heard a TV news report that crime has increased in the city by twenty percent. It's mostly young street gangs, who are mugging people in the subway and on the ferry."

"Well, I'm part of that 20% statistic," admitted Jimmy. "I was mugged in the subway on my way home yesterday."

Mike looked at Jimmy's face and saw the black eye and cuts and said with concern, "You were mugged? They didn't hurt you did they?"

"I'm okay Dad, they gave me a bloody nose and a few bruises when they punched and kicked me. But they didn't get my money or my favorite gold crucifix ring. I fought them off and a cop saved my ass."

Mike, who had been oblivious to information as plain as the nose on Jimmy's face, said passionately, "Yeah, I see. Those bums! Probably drug addicts. The City is full of them. Jimmy, I worry about you when you're drinking, because the muggers see you as an easy target."

"I was not drunk Dad, there were three of them. I need my money. I'm saving for my trip to Italy."

"You were lucky this time," Mike said. "It's good the police arrived in time to help you."

"That's the second time I've been robbed," Jimmy admitted. "Last summer I feel asleep on the subway. A thief sliced my back pocket open with a razor and took my wallet. I was lucky someone found my wallet and mailed it back to me. All the money was missing though."

Jim Anderson said, "You should do what my brother Charlie does. He keeps two wallets on him. One is a giveaway wallet with a few bucks in it. The other has his important papers and cash in it."

"Having an extra 'give-a-way' wallet is a good idea," Mickey said. "You should also keep most of your money in your shoe. This way if you do get mugged again, they won't get it all."

"That's what I would do if I were you, Jimmy," Jim Anderson said.

The three men exchanged worried glances. If there was anybody they knew that could get himself into harm's way, it was Jimmy Zappalorti.

Chapter 17 - Yes, My Friends - Cheers

ON THE FOLLOWING weekend, Jimmy returned to the familiar crowded, smoke-filled Pink Flamingo Club. His piano playing soon had the dance floor filled with couples dancing the night away. Lou Epstein and Don Shepler came through the front entrance and looked up at the stage. Lou pointed to Jimmy at the piano. "There he is Don," Lou said, "That's the fellow who cleaned your chandelier."

Don Shepler was clean-shaven and well-groomed, with a recent haircut. He remembered Jimmy well and wore a new red shirt in the hope that Jimmy would be playing. Lou and Don found an opening in the crowd and walked to the bar. They got the attention of the bartender and ordered drinks. Jimmy completed playing Ray Charles' "Georgia on my Mind." He saw Lou and Don at the bar and waved hello.

Leaning into the microphone, he said, "Well folks, that's the end of this set. I'm taking a short break, but I'll be right back. So don't go anywhere, I'm here 'til three."

Jimmy came down from the stage and waded through the crowd, saying hello to various people and smiling. He made his way to where Lou and Don were standing at the bar.

Lou reached for him, saying, "Hi Jimmy, remember my roommate, Don Shepler?"

Don extended his hand and looked Jimmy in the eyes. "Hello Jimmy. Nice to see you again!" It was apparent to Lou that both men felt an instant attraction for one another.

Jimmy said, "Of course I remember him. Don, I love the way you have your apartment decorated. All the nice antiques, especially the crystal chandelier!"

"Thanks. So, Lou tells me that you work with stained glass."

"Yeah, my older brothers, my father and I make windows for churches and temples."

"No kidding, I've always been interested in stained glass. I just couldn't afford to buy any of the Tiffany stained glass lamps I wanted."

"My brother Mickey makes them, maybe he can make one for you," Jimmy offered. "If you show me what type you want, I can ask him to make one."

Don said, "Really, you think he would do that? That would be wonderful if he could! I would pay him for it, of course."

They made small talk during the break, exchanged compliments, got to know each other better. With a sudden burst of confidence, Jimmy said, "I have a favor to ask. Since I have to play here tomorrow night, I was wondering if I can stay at your place again."

Don answered, winking at him, "Sure you can. You're welcome... anytime."

Lou said with some hope, "The question is, in whose room you will stay?"

Jimmy answered, "Well...I'd like to stay with you, Don."

Lou's facial expression dropped in disappointment. He said, "I respect your choice, Jimmy."

To break the awkward moment, Jimmy excused himself to begin a new set.

Don asked, "Do you know the song 'As Time Goes By'?" The one they used in the film Casablanca?"

"I know most of it. I'll give it a try for you Don," Jimmy said.

Lou sat at the bar and tried to fight his feelings of jealousy. Jimmy and Don kept making eye contact and exchanged smiles from across the room. When The Pink Flamingo closed that night, Don and Jimmy went home together. It was the start of a close relationship that lasted for the rest of their lives.

Chapter 18 - Get the Queer Out of Here!

THE WAGON WHEEL Bar was the only night club in Charleston, Staten Island that offered live entertainment and dancing on weekends, and shuffle board and pool tables during the week. Bobby and Jim Anderson's band, The Careless Five, played there on weekends for the whole summer of 1987. It was owned and managed by one of Bobby's grammar school and high school classmates, Bill Finley. The Wagon Wheel was decorated in Country and Western style. Steer horns hung from the walls, among posters of cowboys roping horses and various rodeo activities. Real wagon wheels were suspended as well, along with bull whips and toy six shooter pistols. There were two full-size pool tables in the back of the bar, usually busy. On a small stage between the bar and the dance floor the band played on weekends. Aside from the local town drunks, the bar was crowded with young single couples and assorted neighborhood men. With the stage empty, music blared from the juke box. Several couples shuffled across the floor.

Jimmy was celebrating his upcoming birthday. He sat at the bar drinking a bottle of Budweiser. Three empty bottles were lined-up in front of him. He was dressed in a gold cowboy shirt, with a black vest, tight blue jeans and black cowboy boots. Two young couples came into the bar. Jimmy recognized his niece, Debbie Zappalorti-Mournet, and her husband, Andy Mournet, along with two friends. As they made their way along the bar, Debbie and Andy saw Jimmy.

After introductions, Jimmy offered to spring for four Coors. He waved to Millie, the bar maid and placed the order. Millie grabbed four bottles of beer from the refrigerator, popped the tops off and placed them on the bar. Jimmy handed her a twenty dollar bill and handed the drinks out.

They all toasted by gently, clicking their bottles together. After a short conversation, Debbie and Andy, and their friends Donna and Steve all went to the dance floor for a slow dance. Jimmy sat at the bar drinking his eighth beer, feeling no pain. The dance floor was crowded. Jimmy watched from the bar as Debbie and Andy, Donna and Steve started fast dancing to The Doors song, "Light My Fire."

The next tune that played from the juke box was Rod Stewart's song: "Do You Think I'm Sexy." Jimmy happened to really like this song, so he staggered up to the stage and started dancing, waving his arms and keeping step to the beat of the music. Jimmy sang along loudly, "Do ya think I'm sexy, do ya want my body, come on sugar let me know." As he sang and danced, he removed his vest first and then his shirt and swung them over his head. Then he kicked off his boots and removed his pants.

Now Debbie, Andy, Donna and Steve along with many others on the dance floor were all laughing hysterically at Jimmy's antics. He threw his pants out to the patrons on the dance floor. At this point, he danced just in his underpants and socks. Everyone on the dance floor and the people at the bar were all laughing at Jimmy, even Millie the bar maid.

Two men not laughing were shooting pool at the rear of the bar. Their names were Michael Taylor and Philip Sarlo. Michael Taylor was a bear of a man: over six-feet tall and nearly 250 pounds. He had long, curly, reddish-brown hair, a mustache and a full beard. He wore a black motorcycle jacket, a green shirt, jeans and black engineer boots. His buddy, Philip Sarlo, was six-foot tall, twenty-six-year old man, who weighed 185-pounds. Sarlo had frizzy, black hair and was clean shaven except for a narrow mustache. He also dressed in black leather, with a red T-shirt, dungarees, and white sneakers.

"Look at that fuckin' faggot," Michael Taylor snorted. "Who wants to see his skinny legs and ass? Throw him outta here!"

"Yeah, get the queer out of here," Philip Sarlo yelled! "Who's the freak?"

Debbie and her friends heard what the two men were yelling. Debbie reacted and said, "He's no freak, that's my Uncle Jimmy. Leave him alone!"

Taylor and Sarlo kept staring at Jimmy and making comments to one another that others could not hear because of the loud music. The manager, Bill Finley, saw and heard what was going on and did not want any trouble in his bar. He picked up Jimmy's vest, shirt and pants.

"Alright Jimmy, you had your fun. Now put your clothes on," Bill ordered. "You had too much to drink. You should go home."

"Why do I have to go home when I'm having fun?" Jimmy countered.

"Because some people in here don't like you undressing," Bill advised. "I don't want any trouble, so I'm asking you nicely: go home now!"

"All right, Bill. Out of respect for you, I'll leave," Jimmy said reluctantly.

Jimmy put his clothes and boots back on and walked towards the door. Taylor and Sarlo stood by the pool table watching him. Michael Taylor yelled in a nasty tone, "Someone should kick the shit out of that fucking faggot. He needs to be taught a lesson!"

114

Chapter 19 - The Best Birthday I Ever Had

FOUR MONTHS LATER, Mike, Sr., Mary, Peggy, Mickey Zappalorti and Jim Anderson were gathered in the kitchen of Zappalorti home. The men sat at the kitchen table while Peggy and Mary fixed sandwiches and drinks.

Mary announced, AI asked Jimmy to come to the house around 12:30 to join us for lunch. It's his birthday, and I made a cake for him."

Mike said, "That's right! Today is September 29th. He's, what, 38 today? I should give him a birthday card. Do you have an extra card, Mom?"

Mary pulled out a box from the cupboard with a stack of blank cards. "Always."

"Thanks, Mary."

"You saved me from embarrassment," Mickey said.

Jim Anderson asked, "Mary, would you have one for me, too? I should give him something."

Mary set a place for Jimmy at the table, finished frosting the cake and decorating it with candles, and then moved it out of sight into the refrigerator. Mike, Mickey and Jim Anderson filled out their cards and each inserted money in them as his gift. The doorbell rang. Peggy answered it.

"Hey! Hi, Peggy. How you been?"

"I'm just fine. Happy birthday, Jimmy."

"Oh, you remembered. Thanks." Jimmy entered the kitchen and looked from face to face, surprised to see everyone standing there. Exclamations of "Happy birthday!" filled the room.

Everyone found a seat at the table and began to eat their lunch. Sandwiches and drinks were passed around the table. After swallowing the last bite of his sandwich, Mike asked, "So, have you been working, Jimmy?"

"Yeah, I have been cutting lawns and doing gardening for people in the neighborhood. I also play piano in the City. With that income, and my Navy pension, I almost have enough saved to afford my trip to Italy."

"Is everyone finished with lunch?" Mary asked.

Mike said, "Time for dessert."

Mary and Peggy cleared the table. Mary went to the refrigerator for Jimmy's birthday cake. Peggy lit all the candles. Jimmy was delighted that so much attention was being paid to him. Mary and Peggy started to sing "Happy birthday to you," and Mike, Mickey and Jim Anderson all joined in.

Jimmy blew out all the candles and beamed with pleasure.

Mary said, "You blew them all out. Your wish will come true."

Jimmy cut the cake into several pieces. He took the first piece for himself, and then served everyone else their pieces. Mary poured coffee for everyone.

Mike playfully pretended to stick his finger up his nose, then into a slice of cake saying, "This is my piece!" which made everyone groan and laugh at his old joke.

They all shared the cake and coffee in a good mood. After finishing his cake, Mike wiped the crumbs from his mouth, took a deep breath, and said, AJimmy, your mother and I have been talking about what happened between you and me last March. I've spoken to Monsignor Finn, our parish priest about this and also did some soul searching. I realize the root of my anger toward you was because I could not accept you as a gay man."

"It's who I am, Dad. I can't change that."

"I understand that now, Jimmy."

Mary said, "We've been talking about this amongst ourselves and Father Finn. He told your Dad that if he loves you he has to accept you for who you are."

Michael paused for a moment, placing his hand on Jimmy's shoulder. "Jimmy, I ask your forgiveness for treating you badly?"

Jimmy stood up, looked down at his father and said, "Dad, of course I forgive you. But, I have my own confession to make. I'm also to blame for us not getting along. I was angry at you for your constant nagging about work. I purposely made noise when I came home at night, just to annoy you and wake you up. So, I also ask for your forgiveness?"

Mike embraced Jimmy. They hugged tenderly. Jimmy's eyes welled up.

He said, "I love you, Daddy."

Mike said, "Love you more, Son. I want you to come back home. Live here with us again."

Mary wiped away a tear. She said, "I prayed for this day, too. You both made me very happy. We're living the Prodigal's Son proverb. Oh, thank God!"

Mickey said, "We want you to come back to work again. We can use your help with the big Saint Thomas church job." Jimmy smiled and nodded, unable to speak.

"Welcome back, Jimmy," Jim Anderson said, and handed him his card. "Here, this is for your birthday. There's some cash in it for you."

Mickey said, "With all this talk, we forgot to give you your birthday cards. Here, Jimmy."

Mary said, "That's right. Here, Jimmy. Happy birthday."

Jimmy sighed, then flashed his most winning smile. "Thanks everyone. This is the best birthday I ever had."

Chapter 20 - Get Lost, Jerks!

ON A WARM sunny afternoon in May 1989, Jimmy gathered his tools to do some landscaping work at a neighbor's house on Androvette Street. He dressed in cut-off jeans, a red cut-off tee-shirt with his stomach showing, black cowboy hat and cowboy boots, an outfit more apropos among The Village People than the Charleston people. He pushed a lawnmower out of the driveway and held a leaf rake centered across the handle of the machine. In his back pocket he had tucked a pair of pruning shears. He stopped to check if he has a full gas tank before going up the street. Five minutes later Jimmy arrived at his destination. He pulled the start-up cord on the mower and began cutting the grass for Mrs. Kaiser.

He pushed the mower straight across the lawn in perfect lines. Mowing slowly back and forth, across the yard as he neatly cut the grass. The lawn mower made wide, smooth low cuts. As Jimmy walked, the neatly trimmed grass had the appearance of a soft green carpet. He also liked the smell of the freshly cut grass.

Farther up Androvette Street two men exited the Deli-Delight grocery store. They were Michael Taylor and Philip Sarlo, the two men who were mocking Jimmy at The Wagon Wheel bar in September of 1988. Both men had a troubled past, arrested in 1986 for gay-bashing. Taylor served 18-months in juvenile detention, while Sarlo was imprisoned for three years. They were charged for kidnap and assault of a gay man they had clubbed with a tire iron, locked in the trunk of his car, and took on a joy ride before crashing the vehicle. Sarlo had a three page rap-sheet for theft.

Taylor and Sarlo had just purchased cigarettes and beer. They were walking back to Michael Taylor's house. As they walked past the yard where Jimmy was doing his landscaping work they stopped to observe him.

"Look Phil, it's that fuckin' queer again parading around in short pants," Taylor said.

"Yeah, Mike, that's him. Let's say something to the fag."

Jimmy made a final sweep, checking as he went that he had not missed any part of the lawn. He came to the edge where the grass met the asphalt pavement. He shut the mower off and moved it onto the driveway, picked up the rake, and started to pull the grass clipping into small piles.

"Who the hell dresses you when you go out?" Taylor asked in a nasty tone. "I wouldn't be caught dead in fag shorts like those."

Surprised, Jimmy turned around to see who was insulting him. Both Michael Taylor and Phil Sarlo stood in the center of Androvette Street, laughing.

"What's your problem," Jimmy asked?

"We don't have a problem, but you sure do," replied Philip Sarlo. "Don't you look in the mirror before you go out?"

"Where can I buy faggot shorts like that?" Taylor asked.

Annoyed now, Jimmy said, "Get lost, jerks! I got work to do.

Taylor said, "Watch your mouth, queer boy!"

"No, you guys better watch your mouths and mind your business," Jimmy said while pointing the rake handle at them.

Surprised that Jimmy did not show any fear, Taylor and Sarlo just laughed and shook their heads. They smirked as they continued walking down Androvette Street towards Taylor's house. Jimmy watched them for a moment, then went back to work raking the grass. He thought to himself that these guys were looking for trouble and that he better not trust them.

Even though Taylor and Sarlo knew Jimmy from The Wagon Wheel bar, this was the first time he had actually encountered them on the street. He sensed they were bad news, but he had no idea how much hatred they held in their hearts. He was too naive and innocent to believe how deeply Taylor and Sarlo's words were borne out of malice and bigotry toward gay men. To him, this was the ignorant and vicious stuff of the Big City, of Manhattan, not of his own quiet home town of Charleston.

Chapter 21 - After All, You're in Rome

AFTER YEARS OF patiently saving his money, Jimmy took his long-anticipated trip to Italy in August of 1988. On his last morning in Rome, he went to Vatican City and joined the crowd of tourists and pilgrims filing through the bronze doors into St. Peter's Basilica. Inside, it was cool and cavernous, and Jimmy's eyes gradually adjusted from the glare of the hot sun outside. His eyes were drawn to the right, to Michelangelo's Pieta, the statue of the Madonna tenderly cradling her dead crucified son in her lap and arms. Jesus' long arms and legs spill limply out of Mary's lap, and his wounds are fresh. Jimmy waited until he could get close to the sculpture and marvel at the smooth marble skin and folds of cloth, all the lifelike details captured in cold, white stone. Mentally, he compared it to Michelangelo's David, which he had seen and admired while in Florence just days before at the Accademia Gallery.

After briefly touring the rest of the Basilica and gazing upward at the huge dome, Jimmy joined the line to file into the Vatican Museum to finally see the Sistine Chapel. The line snaked through decorated antechambers and frescoed halls toward the Holy Father's Chapel with Michelangelo's masterpiece painted on the ceiling. Jimmy struck up a conversation with the elderly couple standing next to him in line.

"I wish my mother and father were here with me," he said. "They always wanted to see these paintings on the ceiling."

The elderly woman said, "Why didn't they come with you?"

"Well, they could not afford to come," Jimmy revealed. "Plus, my father runs his own stained glass business in New York and couldn't take time off from work."

"Oh, that's too bad!"the woman said. "Everyone, especially Roman Catholics should visit the Vatican once in their lifetime."

"Yes I know," Jimmy agreed, Abut it took me more than six years to save enough money for this trip. I'm doing it on a shoestring. I went to Venice, Florence and Genoa last week. Genoa is where my grandfather, Hector Zappalorti, was born."

The elderly man said, "Zappalorti? That's an unusual name."

"I asked a priest in Genoa to look up my family name," Jimmy said. "I found out that a 'zappa' is a kind of farming tool, like a hoe. The priest said my last name means 'One who works the earth.' In other words, a hard worker, a diligent farmer. He said my Italian ancestors were probably good farmers."

The fellow tourists chatted until a man's recorded voice on the public address system intoned: "Visitors to the Vatican, ladies and gentlemen, welcome to the Holy Sistine Chapel!"

As they entered, all eyes gazed upward to the ceiling. The crowd remarked loudly and marveled at the magnificent frescoes. Jimmy's attention was drawn to the huge hand of God on the ceiling. He stared up at it until his neck began to hurt. He felt as if God was reaching down to him, giving him a message. Then he admired the stained glass windows. He felt exhilarated, reborn, happy and alive because of his connection with the amazing artwork of Michelangelo's masterpieces painted on the ceiling. The day was coming to an end, and visitors were asked to leave the building. Jimmy was the last person to walk out, grinning from ear to ear.

Footsore, tired, hungry, but completely happy, Jimmy made his way to a restaurant he had seen that morning. The Da Benito e

Gilberto was a lively place with great food. He enjoyed a leisurely meal in the courtyard, watching the sky deepen from dark blue to purple. On his third glass of Chianti, he started talking with two dark-haired, handsome Italian men at the adjoining table.

The one who identified himself as Gianluca Ginardo asked, "James, me and my friend Luigi would like to buy you another drink. What kind of wine are you drinking?"

Jimmy sounded a bit intoxicated as he answered, "It's Chianti. Not what I usually drink. I like my 'Bud.' The wine is good, but it's going right to my head."

Luigi DeMarco winked at his friend and asked, "What's 'Bud'? I never heard of it."

"Budweiser is a popular American beer in the States," Jimmy replied.

"We're drinking Chianti too," Luigi said. He poured some into Jimmy's glass. "When you're in Rome, you must do as we Romans do. Vino, not Budweiser beer!"

Jimmy smiled and said, "Thanks Luigi, sure I'll have another, but after this I really should get back to my hotel room. I want to tour Rome tomorrow morning."

"Jimmy, you should just relax and enjoy your wine. The night is young," Luigi said.

Gianluca said, "Yes, come to our table and drink with us."

As the night wore on, they spoke of Rome and tourist attractions, churches, stained glass, and of family.

Later that night, very drunk, Jimmy, Gianluca, and Luigi staggered along the street laughing and loudly singing popular Italian songs. They approached a busy intersection.

Jimmy danced with tipsy motions and sang, "When the moon hits your eye like a big pizza pie that's amore."

Without looking, Jimmy stepped onto the street. Luigi saw a speeding cab and tried to grab him and pull him back onto the sidewalk, but was too late. The speeding taxi hit Jimmy, scooping him

126

onto the hood and into the windshield, breaking the glass. The momentum of the impact threw him several feet away as he tumbled to the paved ground. Jimmy lay on the pavement holding his left leg, moaning in pain. Blood dripped from his forehead onto his face. He was not fully conscious.

"Gianluca, run to the coffee shop and call for help," yelled Luigi. "I'll see how he is."

Gianluca sprinted off, crying, "Mama mia, poverino, my poor friend."

Luigi knelt next to Jimmy and held him. "Just lie still Jimmy. Help comes subito."

Jimmy awoke in a white hospital bed ten hours later. He had a full cast on his left leg. A bandage encircled his head, a hydration needle dripped saline into his arm, and there were wires attached to him to monitor life signs. The walls were stark white and unadorned, but for a hanging crucifix. Gianluca and Luigi entered the room with flowers and a fruit basket.

"So, the nurse told us that you have a fractured left leg, several broken ribs, and a mild head concussion," Luigi said. "Aside from that, how you feeling?"

Jimmy rolled his eyes. "I feel lousy. My head hurts, my chest hurts when I breathe, and my leg is throbbing. Anyway, good to see you guys again. I have to call my mother and tell her what happened."

Gianluca assured him, "James, I found her number in your wallet. I called and explained what happened and told her where you are. She wants you to call her. She's worried about you.

I told her you had to stay in the hospital for a few weeks while you heal. Oh, the nurse also asked if you had any health insurance."

"I have my Military Health Coverage," Jimmy answered. "That only pays emergency healthcare, not for any long-term hospital stay. So, I may have to make other arrangements."

Luigi asked, "What kind of arrangements? We only have a small apartment that we share and we both work, so we cannot offer to take you in."

"That's right James, we just don't have the room or the time to care for you," Gianluca said. "It's Sunday and we're off from work, that's why we can visit with you today. Sorry my friend."

Jimmy said, "That's okay, you've done a lot for me already. I'll call my mother and ask her advice. She always has a solution to help me."

Two hours later, the nurse brought Jimmy a telephone and he called home. After explaining what was going on and his dilemma with the hospital bill, Jimmy said, "Mom, the nurse said unless I sign the papers agreeing to pay for my stay at the hospital, I have to leave by tomorrow."

"Your father and I can't afford to pay three-hundred dollars a day for your stay there. We'll have to think of something else."

"What else can I do Mom? Ask for charity?" Jimmy suggested.

Mary exclaimed, "That's a good idea! Find out if the Sisters of Charity have a convent there in Vatican City. If they do, get the phone number and ask if they'll take you in while you recuperate."

Later that day, via an English telephone book, Jimmy found the number for the Sisters of Charity near Vatican City. He dialed the number and eventually connected with a Sister Maria. While working through various rules and regulations, especially concerning ability to pay, Jimmy mentioned that his Aunt Regina Ryan was a nun in their order. The connection provided the magic acceptance, and it was arranged to have an ambulance to pick him up the next morning.

Shortly after hanging up the phone, Jimmy was visited by attorney Antonio DeVito, who assured him that he had a legitimate case and might stand to win as much as 50,000,000.00 lira. All that would be necessary was to sign a Power of Attorney. After Jimmy finished signing all the documents DeVito finally informed Jimmy of one particular clause in the document.

"Of course I would get one half of whatever you are awarded," DeVito said casually.

"One half! That seems like too much."

"No James, that's the standard attorney fee for Italy," DeVito lied.

"Well, I guess whatever money I get will be more than I expected," Jimmy said.

DeVito assured him of the same and walked out of the room wearing an enormous grin.

Chapter 22 - Jimmy and the Pink Panthers

IT TOOK TWO weeks for Jimmy to recover well enough to travel back home to Staten Island. Mickey picked him up at Newark Airport and Jimmy was finally home from his extended stay in Rome, through the kindness of the Sisters of Charity. It was three months before he heard from the Italian attorney, Antonio DeVito who kept Jimmy in the dark about the case. On June 13, 1989, Jimmy, Don, Lou and another friend, Frank Quinn were having dinner at the Stonewall Inn restaurant, which is located on Christopher Street, between 7th Avenue South and Waverley Place in Manhattan.

The Stonewall Inn was notorious for the confrontations between hundreds of gay men and the New York City Police department back on the night of Friday, June 17, 1969. This tavern was, in fact, the birthplace of gay activism in New York, when a group of regulars made a historic stand against raiding police officers, later known as the Stonewall Uprising. Originally, a private club, but it became a public restaurant, a favorite drinking and party spot for local residents and tourists.

Two friends of the Zappalorti family, Bert Coffman and Bruce Kogan, were there that night at the Stonewall Inn and were among the original protestors back in 1969. The wine flowed, the table conversation was stimulating, but Jimmy wanted to see a new cop film called The Thin Blue Line. Jimmy and Don left together. They walked down Bleaker Street in the Village, where the streets were filled with vehicles and the sidewalks were filled with people. Jimmy and Don held hands as they walked. As they approached a busy intersection they had to stop for a red traffic light. They were in conversation as they waited for it to change.

Loitering against a storefront building was a group of skinhead gang bangers. One of them alerted his friends to the gay couple. The five punk gang bangers surrounded Jimmy and Don. One spoke in a high, effeminate voice.

"Say, somebody, can you tell me where I can catch the Forty Second Street Fairy?"

The five gang bangers all laughed. Jimmy and Don just looked at them with resentment.

A second punk askew, "Are you guys members of the Fudge Packer Society?"

All five punks all burst into laughter, and a third one jumped in on the mocking.

"You fags want to suck a Creamsicle?"

Jimmy had enough. "Shut up and get lost!"

The first punk asked, "Who's gonna make us?"

Without showing any fear, Jimmy looked him in the eyes and said, "We are, you little shits!"

One of the gang sucker punched Jimmy from the side, hitting him in the face. The others piled on Jimmy and Don. Jimmy went after the punk that hit him first, aiming for his mouth, he threw a punch. The punk goes down.

Within seconds, a relatively quiet corner of Manhattan had erupted into a full-blown melee. The night air suddenly filled with the loud noise of tweeting police whistles. Surprised, everyone stopped fighting. Jimmy and Don looked around to see nine members of the Pink Panthers, a civilian patrol, blowing their police whistles. Their uniform was black tee-shirts with a pink cat's paw on the front and, on the back, the words Pink Panthers.

The vigilantes grabbed and overpowered the five gang bangers.

Within moments, two police cars pulled up with red roof lights flashing. Four cops arrested and handcuffed the five street punks. They took sworn statements about the incident from Don, with his bloody nose, Jimmy, with a welt on his face, and the Pink Panther witnesses.

In reaction to a series of intolerance-based attacks and murders, a group of New York City gay men and lesbian woman started the citizen protection patrol called the Pink Panthers. Armed only with whistles and walkie-talkies, their members patrolled the streets of Greenwich Village. If they witnessed any form of anti-gay violence or other crimes, they would call the police and take accurate descriptions of the perpetrators.

The group adopted the footprint of a cat's paw in a pink triangle on a black tee-shirt as their logo and colors. The logo resembled the MGM-Pathe Communications Company's intellectual property from the movie The Pink Panther. On January 8, 1991, MGM sued to block the New York homosexual protection patrol from using the name and trademarked paw design. The lawsuit also sought unspecified damages in excess of $100,000. On October 5, 1991, MGM studios won. The Federal judge who heard the case said that Athe community patrol, which seeks to stop anti-gay violence, had infringed on MGM's Pink Panther trademark," which was used in eight movies and in a cartoon series. "MGM uses its trademark to promote an image of lighthearted, nonpolitical, asexual, amicable, comic entertainment," Judge Pierre N. Leval wrote. "The Pink Panthers Patrol's use of the name is associated with political activism, violence, defiance, homosexuality and angry confrontation." The judge said the public could be confused into thinking that the patrol and the Pink Panther cartoon character were somehow related. The safety patrol group's lawyer, Evan Wolfson of the Lambda Legal Defense and Education Fund, advised them to change their name. So, the group tweaked the name with a slight hard 'A' Boston accent and called themselves the "Pink Panthas."

Chapter 23 - You've Got a Friend

AFTER JIMMY RETURNED from Italy, he remained restless. He returned to his routines of working with stained glass, playing piano in Greenwich Village, helping the neighbors with yard work, but his primary focus was on building his shack. A key part of the project was installing a small wooden boardwalk across a wetland on the trail to the beach. The section would flood during rainstorm events and was always muddy. A high stand of Phragmites reeds grew on both sides of the path. With help from Don and Lou, the boardwalk got done. After that, he could get to his beach side shack without getting his feet wet or muddy during any kind of weather. Once past the reeds it was impossible to see any other houses, so Jimmy could indulge his fantasies of being the king of his own small isolated hideaway.

To get to his beach house, Jimmy crossed Androvette Street from his parents' home, cut through the driveway in Owen Reiter's' yard, went through a patch of woods and the Phragmites reeds, up a slight incline, and out to an open sandbar. A few more minutes of walking on the sand path brought him to a small bluff, with a sweeping view of the Arthur Kill River. To the north, the river connected Newark Bay and the Kill Van Kull to the Lower New York Harbor, and, farther to the east, the Atlantic Ocean. The opposite shore from Jimmy's shack was dotted with oil refineries, industrial sites and factories. The shore of the river was blighted by a panorama of rotting wood and metal boats and barges, but this place on the river considered of no value by the rest of the world provided Jimmy with the privacy he craved. Jimmy liked to retreat there at the end of a working day, drinking beer and reading. It also became a favorite place to host parties for friends. One such party was celebrated in July 1989 when Jimmy's brother, Robert, Sr. and nephew Robert, Jr. visited. All three were in conversation as they walked the trail toward the beach shack. Jimmy carried two six-packs of Budweiser beer and Robert, Jr. toted his guitar.

Bobby asked, "Jimmy, you said your friends from the City are already at your beach house. Who are they?"

"Well, my good friend Don Shepler is here," Jimmy replied. "His two buddies, Lou and Frank, are also here. They're cooking up some chicken and burgers on the grill for us. They came here yesterday and helped clean up the beach. We drank beers and watched the sunset last night. We had a good time."

Robert Sr. asked, "Is Don the guy you've told me about? The interior decorator from Manhattan you're involved with?"

"Yeah, he's a great guy. We get along so well," Jimmy said. "He's a nice guy with a good sense of humor."

Introductions were made, and the general mood was easy and expansive. When the food was ready, beers and Pepsis provided the liquid refreshment. Jimmy related how he had finally received $2,123.00 as his settlement payment for the Rome taxi accident. The general consensus was that, between the charges the lawyer subtracted his time, expenses, and court costs from the award, plus the agreed-upon fifty percent, Jimmy had been badly bamboozled.

While he ate, Bobby looked around. "Uncle Jimmy, you really fixed-up your beach house nicely."

"It's looked nicer. Last month someone wrecked it on me and broke some of the windows. Don and Lou helped me clean it up, and your grandfather and Mickey helped me replace all the broken glass.

They made me a clear stained glass window for my bedroom."

Robert, Sr. asked, "Did you find out who trashed the place?"

"No," Jimmy said. "I don't know who did it. It's not local teenagers, because I know most of them. They even helped me build the dock and the brick path, so it's not them. I'm just not sure who wrecked it on me. Maybe it's someone from Charleston somewhere. I don't know."

"Well it's a damn shame they trashed your hut," Robert declared.

A few casual snapshots were taken of the group. After that Bobby picked up his guitar. Frank asked him, AHey Bobby, do you know the song by Carole King, the one that James Taylor made famous, 'You've Got a Friend'?"

Bobby said, "Yeah! Uncle Jimmy recently gave me a songbook with that tune in it. I hope I can remember all the chords. Everyone, sing along with me. Here goes."

Bobby positioned his fingers on the first chord, took his pick and played the introduction to the song. When he gave them a cue, Frank, Robert, Jimmy, Don, and Lou began to sing the lyrics in unison. Six people swayed to the rhythm of the music. Lou joked around, singing into the end of a broom handle as if it were a microphone.

"All you have to do is call, and I'll be there. Yeah, yeah, yeah. You've got a friend..."

For all the fun they were having, it could have been a party of the rich and famous on a secluded beach in Tahiti.

136

Chapter 24 - I Have Gifts for Your Kids

AUTOMOBILE TRAFFIC ON the Garden State Parkway was extremely heavy on Christmas Eve as people rushed to their holiday destinations. Robert, Sr. and his two sons, Robert, Jr. and Michael were on their way from Beachwood, New Jersey to visit his parents, Mike and Mary and his brother Jimmy for the holiday. Because of the large volume of travelers, traffic was backed up for a mile at the toll booths of the Outerbridge Crossing. Robert was resigned to the holiday snare; he always made a point to see his parents and Jimmy during Christmas, to exchange presents and catch-up on the Zappalorti family news.

Christmas was Jimmy's favorite season and time of the year. Mary took much pleasure in decorating the house and placing the Nativity statues and manger under the tree. As her health failed, Jimmy took over those tasks for her. He also enjoyed decorating both the inside and the outside of the house with sparkling, colored lights. He would illuminate the outside display every night, just before dark. The final touch was to play Christmas music on the Motorola record player. As part of the living room decorations, Jimmy placed Mickey's old electric train set around the base of the Christmas tree.

When visitors would come to the house he turned on the transformer, so the train would slowly roll around the tracks. Then he'd press the switch to make the locomotive sound its soft whistle.

After demonstrating how well the old set worked, he would then show off his brown, silver and gold cuckoo clock that hung on the living room wall.

By 1985, Mary' emphysema prevented her from doing much shopping. Instead, she gave Christmas cards with cash to all her children and grandchildren. Mike, Sr. was not good at picking out gifts or shopping, so Mary would always make a gift list of items for him to purchase and for whom. Mike would go to the stores to do his Christmas shopping, purchase the items Mary had suggested and bring them back for her inspection.

Jimmy's duty was to wrap all the presents with colorful paper and fancy bows. Mike would follow Mary's list to the letter, but afterwards he would proudly take credit for purchasing such nice gifts for his family members. In turn, Mary would smile at her husband with satisfaction and let him take the credit for being thoughtful. Mary always said, "It's better to give than to receive." She truly believed the words and lived by them.

Robert and his two sons arrived at his parents' decorated home at 4:30 P.M. The large spruce tree and three small cedar trees in the front yard were all brightly illuminated with colorful Christmas lights. They carried shopping bags filled with presents to the front door and rang the bell. Robert carried his new video camera, so he could take pictures of his parents and Jimmy. Jimmy opened the wreath-covered door and greeted his brother and two nephews.

"Merry Christmas! Hi, Bobby! Robert, Michael, come on in," greeted Jimmy with a big, cheerful smile. "Come in the living room and see the tree. Put your coats on the hooks in the hall while I turn on the electric train."

The Christmas tree was lit, the Nativity scene sat atop the piano surrounded by small white lights. "Silent Night" played on the Victrola. After removing their coats, Roberts senior and junior. and Michael admired the Christmas tree.

Mike, Sr. came out from the back bedroom, "Hi, guys! Merry Christmas! Come on in the back; your Mother wants to see you."

The gathering walked through the dining room and into Mary's back bedroom. Mary sat in her reclining chair to the left of her bed. She wore her pink flowered pajamas and a new white bathrobe Mike had just given her for Christmas. Her face lit-up when she saw so many of her boys. Hugging went on for some time.

Mike asked Michael, "What do you have there in the leather case?"

"It's my Dad's new video camera. We're going to take a video of you, Nana and Jimmy."

"Oh yeah, let's see it," replied Mike. Michael handed the camera case to his Father.

"Here Dad, show Pop the camera."

The men took turns using the camera as presents were opened. Mike got a dark brown winter coat. Mary unwrapped three large crossword puzzle books with delight, followed by a big box of her favorite candy: marzipans. Each piece of almond paste was molded into miniature shapes of colorful fruit.

Then Bobby then reached into the shopping bag and took out two more presents, these wrapped in green paper with red bows.

"Here, Jimmy. These are for you from me and the boys. Merry Christmas!"

Jimmy's was surprised that he was given two presents. He neatly pulled off the paper of the smaller box, so it did not tear apart. Then he opened the first box, revealing a light tan shirt with a gold silk tie. Everyone knew how partial Jimmy was to the color gold. Jimmy carefully unwrapped the second gift. As he pulled the box open his expression showed surprise. It was a brown sports jacket with gold buttons, so match the shirt and tie.

"I'll wear it all on New Year's Eve," Jimmy decided.

While more presents were opened, Robert Sr. said, "We're going to Peggy's house after we leave here, so you can give your holiday wishes to everyone on the video camera. I'll tape you then play it at Peggy's house when we get there."

When it was Jimmy's turn to offer a holiday greeting, he just stood there thinking of what to say. A moment later he said into the camera lens, "Merry Christmas everybody. Peggy and Richie, I miss you." He turned to Bobby, "Can I play a song on the piano for them?"

"Sure you can. Go ahead into the living room, I'll follow you." Jimmy walked into the living room, sat on the piano stool and started to play "Silent Night."

After playing half of the song, Jimmy looked at the camera and smiled. Then he played "Rudolf the Red Nosed Reindeer," and sang along with it. When he finished, he stood up and took a bow, then said, "Merry Christmas and Happy New Year everybody."

Bobby stopped recording and said, "That was good Jimmy. You put on a nice show and I have it all on videotape."

"Can I see it," Jimmy asked?

Bobby replied, "Do you have a video cassette player?"

"No, we don't have one," replied Jimmy sadly.

"Next time you come to my house, I'll show it to you, Jimmy. Remind me, okay. Now, go stand in front of the Christmas tree and I'll get a shot of you there," Bobby said.

Jimmy walked over to the tree and put on his winning smile. He always enjoyed being filmed and being in the spotlight. He waved at the camera lens and said loudly, "Merry Christmas everybody!"

Neither Jimmy, nor Robert could have ever imagined that December 24, 1989, was the last Christmas they'd spend together. Even worse, it was the last time that Robert would ever see his little brother alive again. The videotape he shot that day had a portion of the footage accidentally erased, because the cassette was not properly labeled. Only a small portion of Jimmy smiling in front of the Christmas tree and playing the piano remain. Nevertheless, the footage that does remain is treasured because Robert and other family members can watch it and see Jimmy smiling from ear to ear. That's the way they like to remember him.

Chapter 25 - It Takes One to Know One

ON JANUARY 22, 1990, it was a mild winter afternoon. Jimmy walked out of the Deli Delight store on Androvette Street carrying a bag of groceries. He stopped and placed the bag on a bench in front of the store. He reached into the bag and took out a pack of cigarettes, opened it, lit one up, and took a drag. At that point, he noticed three guys seated on the porch of the Wagon Wheel Bar, a neighborhood bar across the street. Jimmy recognized two of them as Michael Taylor and Phillip Sarlo, the guys who had harassed him in the past. Taylor made a snide remark about Jimmy to the others and they all laughed. Jimmy did not hear exactly what was said, but he did not like their behavior.

Jimmy looked at them and said, "What's so funny?"

Taylor answered, "You are! Who taught you how to walk?"

"If you don't like the way I walk, don't look," Jimmy said.

Sarlo said, "Well, we can't miss you when you strut past." He stood up and did a crude, effeminate, mockery of Jimmy. Taylor and the other two men laughed.

Jimmy said, "I'm sick and tired of you guys always making fun of me."

Taylor glanced at his friends for support, then said nastily, "Well, get the fuck out of our sight, and we won't call you names."

He said defiantly, "My family has lived in this town since 1950. I have a right to walk on this street any time I feel like it. You guys are the outsiders, not me."

"Yeah, well, now we live in this town too, so shut the fuck up!" Sarlo said.

"Ah, lemme alone, you creeps." Jimmy picked up his bag of groceries. "I don't have to take any verbal abuse from the likes of you." He started to walk away.

Taylor stood up and performed a crude, effeminate, imitation of the way Jimmy walked. Then he began by imitating, "I don't have to take any verbal abuse. You're a fuckin' faggot." Jimmy said defensively, "It takes one, to know one...jerks!"

Sarlo yelled, "You better shut your face you queer bastard!" Sarlo took a step down off the porch toward him and said, "You're just asking for an ass-whipping, faggot."

Jimmy stood his ground "I'm not scared of you!"

Angry, Taylor and Sarlo started to walk across the street toward Jimmy. They were yelling so loudly that the woman clerk inside the Deli Delight could hear their ugly words through the glass storefront.

A police car pulled up in front of the deli. Taylor and Sarlo stopped, turned around, and walked back to the front of the bar. Unaware of what was going on, the cop emerged from his patrol car and walked into the deli to buy a cup of coffee. Once the police officer was inside, Taylor told Jimmy, "You're so lucky that cop came along you fuckin' fag. We'll see you another time and make you eat those words."

Jimmy grinned at them and started walking down the street towards his home. Taylor and Sarlo angrily watched him go. Jimmy ignored them and started to walk down the street towards his house. The two thugs' eyes followed Jimmy down Androvette Street. Taylor and Sarlo walked back onto the Wagon Wheel porch then sat around aimlessly. A wintry breeze began to flow as night approached. The leafless trees along Androvette Street swayed in a perpetual hula against the dark winter sky.

Chapter 26 - Mary, Your Dinner Is Served

INSIDE THE ZAPPALORTI residence, Michael, Sr. fixed dinner in the kitchen for his invalid wife Mary, who was lying in her downstairs bedroom at the rear of the house. At 5:00 P.M. he heard Jimmy's key in the front door lock. The family dog, Blacky, jumped up, barked, and ran to the front room.

Mike said, "Quiet Blacky, it's only Jimmy. What took you so long? Did you get the seedless rye bread for your mother?"

By then, Jimmy had put the incident with Taylor and Sarlo out of his mind. He placed the grocery bag down on the kitchen table and started to unpack it. He looked at his father and answered, "Yes, Dad, I got what you wanted. I also got myself cigarettes and a six pack of Bud."

"Open the bread and butter two slices for your mother, while I finish cooking these lamb chops," Mike asked.

"I'm just going to say hello to mom first."

In her dark, wood-paneled room, Mary was sitting up in bed. An oxygen tank hissed softly under the cluttered end table. She had a tube feeding air into her nostrils. Mary's long brown hair was streaked with grey.

"Jimmy, you were gone for awhile. What kept you?"

"Oh, I was talking to Carol Kosa on the way up the street," Jimmy said. "Then I stopped for a cigarette when I was leaving the grocery store."

Jimmy did not tell his parents or anyone else about the verbal confrontation with Taylor and Sarlo. He did not want to worry his mother and just kept the incident to himself. He helped his mother to the bathroom, then assembled her dinner on a tray. First, however, he thoughtfully placed a rose in a bud vase. He allowed his father to bring the tray to the bedroom. When she asked if he was the one who thought to bring the rose.

Mike said jokingly, "Why, of course I did, my dear. Nothing but the best for the 'Lady of the House.'"

"Well, thank you for being so thoughtful. Now go fix yourself a plate, then join me," Mary said.

All three Zappalortis ate in the bedroom. The television was on and all three watched the evening news as they ate their dinner. They finished their meals and began to chat.

"Are you going to your Al-Anon meeting tonight Mike," asked Mary?

"I am. I'm sponsoring a new member tonight, his name is John Campbell. I asked him to come in a half hour early, so I can explain the rules and what's expected of him. I should leave here soon."

Mary asked, "Is it his wife that has the drinking problem?"

"Yeah, she has been drinking for the past three years but has finally joined Alcoholics Anonymous,"

"What about you Jimmy? What are you doing tonight?"

Jimmy said, ASince the weather is so mild tonight, I think I'll just go down to my Beach House and relax, drink my beer and finish reading that John Godey book The Taking of Pelham, 1-2- 3."

"Are you going to stay there all night, or will you be coming back home," Mary asked?

"No, I should be back around 10:30 P.M., probably before Daddy gets home." Jimmy turned and said to his father, "You can go to your meeting, Dad. I'll clean up and put the dishes in the dishwasher before I go."

"Okay, thanks Jimmy. I'm just about ready," Mike said. He leaned over and kissed his wife. "Mary, I'll see you later. Come on, Blacky."

Darkness had now set in and it was just after 6:00 P.M. Mike and his dog came out the front door of the house, and they walked to the grassy field next door so Blacky could do his business. After a minute they both walked to the family car parked in the driveway. Mike opened the passenger door and let Blacky jump in the front seat. The family dog sat up like a person on the passenger seat as he always did. Mike backed out and began to pull away. Just then, Jimmy came out the front door with his six-pack of Budweiser, he stopped and waved goodbye to his Father. Mike smiled at his son, acknowledged him with a nod and drove up Androvette Street and out of view.

Jimmy crossed Androvette Street, walking past the Reiter's yard, to the familiar sand road to his shack. He walked across the wooden planks that he had placed over the mud and soon came to the open sandbar. The full moon was partially hidden by thick clouds. He walked across the sandbar, unlocked the front door of his cabin, and stepped inside.

As he went in, a gush of wind slammed the door closed. A horseshoe Jimmy had nailed up above the door for good luck vibrated and one of the nails on the right loosened and fell out. The horse shoe slipped around into the upside down position. A moment later, an orange light flickered through the shack's windows from the oil lamp and candles that Jimmy had just lit.

Chapter 27 - I Said We'd Get Ya

MICHAEL ZAPPALORTI SR. continued up Androvette Street. As he drove past the Wagon Wheel Bar, he noticed two men standing on the front porch. Michael did not know that Phillip Sarlo and Michael Taylor had been in a confrontation with his youngest son a few hours earlier. Because it was now dark and the car drove past quickly, Phillip Sarlo thought he saw two people in the car. He said, "Hey, wasn't that the faggot's father and mother that just drove past? That means the queer's home alone."

Michael Taylor answered, "Yeah, it was them. Let's go see if we can find him."

The two men walked down the dark street and stopped in front of the Zappalorti house. They looked around but did not hear or see any activity. Sarlo walked up the stairs and tried to open the front door.

"It's locked. Looks like no one's home."

"Yeah, the house is dark," Taylor agreed. "We should check to see if he went down to his shack."

Jimmy was resting comfortable in his shack. The cabin was lit by two oil lamps, a Coleman lantern and several candles. A kerosene stove burned, providing sufficient heat to warm the entire cabin. Jimmy used to have a potbelly stove that he liked, but the ones who had wrecked his shack stole it. The kerosene stove was easier, because he didn't have to chop wood, just pour in the fuel. Because it was very warm and comfortable in the shack, Jimmy had removed his shirt and pants and was lying on top of the bedspread, in his underwear and tee-shirt. He took a drag on his cigarette, sipped some beer as he continued reading the novel.

Sarlo and Taylor walked down the long dark path with only the aid of the moonlight. As they crossed the sandbar, they saw lights in the windows of Jimmy's shack. The only other signs of life were the distant lights of the New Jersey shoreline across the river, a tugboat pulling an oil tanker ship to Port Mobil and the distant sound of automobile traffic on the Outerbridge Crossing.

Sarlo said, "Good, he's here at the shack, I hope he's alone."

Taylor whispered, "Keep your voice down, I don't want him to hear us coming. I want the advantage of surprise."

"He can't hear us, don't worry."

They walked slowly around the back of the shack, towards the large stained glass picture window that faced the river. Taylor peered in from the edge and saw Jimmy reading on the bed.

"It looks like he's alone," Taylor whispered.

Sarlo answered, "Let's go around to see if the door is unlocked. Then we can barge in and kick his ass."

The two men moved stealthily around the shack to the front door. Taylor reached with his right hand and turned the door knob. It opened. They boldly entered the front room of the cabin. Jimmy heard the sound of the door scraping open. He looked up and was shocked to see the two men forcefully entering. Jimmy jumped to his feet and shouted, "What are you doing? Get the hell out of here!"

Taylor closed in quickly and punched Jimmy, saying, "I said we would get ya!"

Jimmy staggered back to the bed from the force of the blow but tried to get back up to defend himself. Sarlo grabbed Jimmy's feet and tried to pull him off the bed. Jimmy kicked his hands loose, then kicked Taylor in the balls. Taylor arched over holding his crotch. Jimmy got up and hit Sarlo in the face with his fist.

Taylor grunted in pain, "You fucking faggot, you're going to pay for that."

Jimmy yelled, "Get out of my house! Get out now!"

He stood ready to fight. Sarlo and Taylor angrily rushed Jimmy at the same time. They pummeled him in the face and body. Taylor grabbed Jimmy's tee-shirt by the collar and ripped it completely off his back. Sarlo punched Jimmy in the face, knocking him down. They both kicked him with their boots until Jimmy was unconscious.

Sarlo stood over Jimmy, gasping for breath. "You queer bastard, told you we were gonna kick the shit out of you. Looks like he's out Mike."

"Yeah," Taylor echoed, "the faggot's eaten his words like I said."

He wiped the blood from his lip and looked around the shack. He spotted the Budweiser beer on the kitchen table.

"Hey Phil, let's drink some of his beer." They moved into the kitchen and sat at the table. Taylor continued, "That felt good."

"Yeah, it did," Sarlo agreed, "Gimme a beer. Let's see if he has any money in his wallet, then we get the fuck out of here."

In the other room, Jimmy slowly woke up but pretended to be unconscious. He heard what they said about his wallet and taking his money. Jimmy remembered he had placed his wallet on the end table by the bed. Then he looked at the baseball bat that he kept in the corner for protection. He quickly jumped up, took his wallet from the end table and then grabbed the baseball bat. He came through the bedroom door with the bat over his shoulder ready to swing.

Jimmy yelled, "Now get the hell out of here or I'll use this bat!"

Surprised, Taylor said, "Holy shit, the faggot's got some fight left in him."

"Fuck you," Taylor said in anger. There was a confusion of movement and sound. Jimmy cracked Sarlo on his head, knocking him down; and then with an upward jab, hit Taylor in the gut with the end of the bat. Taylor had the wind knocked out of him. This gave Jimmy a chance to run out the front door. Sarlo ran after him, caught up to him and tackled Jimmy, knocking him down on the sand path.

Because Jimmy was holding both his wallet and the bat, he did not have a good grip on the bat. It fell away from his reach when they landed on the ground. Jimmy stood and tried to grab the bat. Sarlo quickly grabbed him from behind and held him.

Angry, Taylor came out the cabin door with an open, five-inch folding knife in his hand. As Taylor approached Jimmy he demanded, "Give us your wallet you fucking queer bastard!"

"I'm not giving you anything," Jimmy yelled.

With all his strength, Jimmy threw his wallet into the bushes off the path. Sarlo grabbed both his arms from behind and held them tightly. Taylor was really pissed now and said, "How do you like this, you queer bastard?" He took the five-inch knife and plunged it into Jimmy's bare chest. He pulled it out and then stabbed the knife into Jimmy's stomach.

Jimmy screamed in shock and pain. He started to cough and some blood dripped from his mouth.

Sarlo gasped, "Holy shit, Mike! I didn't think you were going to stab him!"

Jimmy coughed again, "Stop..."

Sarlo still held Jimmy's arms behind his back. He said, nervously, "Let's get the hell out of here, Mike."

Mike Taylor was breathing hard. He said coldly and without emotion, "No, Phil, I'm gonna finish this fuckin' fag off."

"Jesus Christ, Mike, you're talking murder!"

Sarlo released his grip and Jimmy fell to the ground. Blood dripped from his mouth.

Groaning in severe pain, he started praying, "God help me. Hail Mary, full of grace, the Lord is with thee. Blessed art Thou among women. Blessed is the fruit of thy womb, Jesus..."

Taylor said, "Shut the fuck up. No one can help you now."

Taylor grabbed Jimmy by the hair, pulled his head backward, and deeply cut his throat from ear to ear. The blade of the knife caused

Jimmy extreme pain. He moved his mouth to talk, but only his lips moved and his voice could not be heard. His lips muttered, "God... help... me!

Taylor then took his knife and stabbed Jimmy again in the stomach and two more times in the chest. Shocked, Sarlo looked down at Jimmy on the ground and slowly backed away from the bloody, dying body.

Taylor looked down at Jimmy and said, "Now, that's what you get when you fuck with me, you queer bastard."

Sarlo's voice was tight with fear. "Now what the hell are we going to do Mike?"

"Let's find his wallet and get his money," Taylor said.

Sarlo started searching the ground. "He threw it over this way somewhere, but I can't see much without a light. See if you can find a flashlight in the shack."

"Okay, be right back." Taylor went into the cabin. He saw Jimmy's jacket hanging on the back of a chair. Felt in the pockets and found a set of keys. Taylor took them and placed them in his jacket pocket. Then he looked in the bedroom and saw a flashlight on the end table. He grabbed the flashlight and went back outside.

"I found a flashlight, Phil."

"Good, because I'm getting nowhere fast. I think it went in here someplace. Shine the light here." They stumbled around for a few minutes, but couldn't find the wallet even with the flashlight.

Taylor said, "Phil, I think we should take his body and dump it in the river. The tide will take him out into the Atlantic Ocean, and no one will ever find him."

"That's probably a good idea. If they can't find a body, they can't pin anything on us."

"Come on Phil give me a hand. Let's get rid of him."

The two men walked back out onto the path where Jimmy's body lay. They grabbed him by his arms and dragged him face down towards the river, leaving a broken trail of blood in the sand. They pulled him along the narrow path and down the steps, to the beach. There was a small dock to the left of the stairs that Jimmy had built for his row boat. They dragged Jimmy's corpse up onto the dock.

Taylor directed, "Grab his feet, Phil, so we can throw him into the water."

Sarlo suggested, "Maybe we should bury him under that old boat over there."

"No, we don't have shovels to bury him!" Taylor said. "Let's just throw him in the river and the tide will take him out."

"Okay, give me a chance to get a good grip on him."

"You ready?" Taylor asked. "Swing him in."

Taylor had Jimmy's arms and Sarlo had his feet. They swung the body and threw it into the water. Jimmy landed on his back, face up. The water caused the blood from his wounds to flow freely again. His blood mingled with the salt water, turning it red as Jimmy's body slowly bobbed up and down. The blood and water formed a shimmering halo around Jimmy's head. The moonlight gave him a surreal martyred saint aspect. As he floated there, Jimmy's left arm happened to tangle on a rope that he had tied to the dock when he built it, just in case he ever needed it. As it turned out, in his death he needed it. The tangled rope kept his body floating in place, pale and still, instead of floating out into the river where it may not have been found for days, weeks, or ever.

The two murderers trudged back towards the shack. They made another, intensive search for the wallet in the bushes where Jimmy had thrown it.

"I found keys in his jacket," Taylor announced. "If we can't find the wallet, we should check his house. Maybe we can find some cash or jewelry there."

Sarlo said, "I'm gonna look for the wallet again. It's got to be here somewhere."

"Okay, while you're doing that, I'm gonna look around the shack."

Neither of the two men found anything of value or worth taking in the shack, so they stopped looking and walked back to the Zappalorti home on Androvette Street.

Chapter 28 - Give Me Jimmy's Keys

AT 9:00 P.M. on January 22, 1990, 75-year old Mary Zappalorti was resting in her downstairs back bedroom. She wore white flannel flowered print pajamas. She sat-up in bed watching television. Mary was not aware that her youngest son had just been murdered. She enjoyed watching her favorite TV shows in the evening while her husband Mike was at his Al-Anon meetings. Michael organized Al-Anon meeting each week at local churches and community centers and attended these group discussions three nights a week. Mary suffered from chronic emphysema, brought on by years of smoking Camel cigarettes. Whenever she walked around the house too far, she suffered from shortness of breath and sometimes needed oxygen tank to help her breathe.

Mary could neither go out much anymore nor climb the stairs, so Michael gave up his butterfly museum and collection and moved his wife's bedroom to the downstairs portion of the home. Sometimes Mike would take the family dog Blacky with him to his meetings. On this night, Blacky went with Mike to wait in the car while he led the Al-Anon group discussion. Mary was completely alone.

After throwing Jimmy's body into the Arthur Kill River, Michael Taylor and Philip Sarlo went back to the Zappalorti residence to steal cash and jewelry. The house was still dark, and the car was gone. After checking that no neighbors were around and the street was deserted, they tried one of Jimmy's keys in the front door lock. It

158

didn't fit, but the next one slid in and unlocked the door. They walked into the front foyer.

"Now what?" Sarlo whispered. "Should we look upstairs first?"

"Yeah," Taylor answered. "Let's find his bedroom and see what's there."

Both men slowly and quietly walked up the stairway like two hyenas looking for a meal. They reached the top of the stairs on the second floor. A night light dimly illuminated the hallway. They saw three separate bedroom doors, the one directly in front of them locked with a padlock and hasp. Walking towards Mike's bedroom, Taylor said, "Let's check the open rooms, Phil."

They went into Mike's room first, flipping the light switch on and ransacking the drawers. Taylor saw a black leather case in a tray on top of Mike's dresser. He opened it and saw that it was a gold Eucharist set.

"Hey, Phil, this looks like it's worth something," Taylor said, stuffing it into his pocket. "It's gold."

Sarlo said, "Good, see anything else of value?"

Taylor pulled open an end table drawer. "Hey, here's some cash. Looks like about a hundred bucks!" he said excitedly.

"Great, we can use it. Give me the keys, so I can unlock the other bedroom door," Sarlo said.

Taylor tossed Sarlo the keys as he walked from the room. He went to Jimmy's door and fumbled with the keys trying to open the lock. None seem to fit.

"Dammit Mike, I can't get this lock open," Sarlo complained.

"There must be something valuable in there, otherwise why would it be locked?" Taylor reasoned.

"None of the fucking keys fit. I tried them all twice. Let's just force the thing open," Sarlo said.

Taylor took the keys and tried to unlock the door without success. Taylor gave the keys back to Sarlo, who placed them in his jacket pocket. The two men set their shoulders on the door and began to push, but the hasp and lock held. They tried again, with no luck. Angry, Taylor stepped back and kicked the door forcefully with his right foot. He broke the wooden molding away from the hasp that was holding the lock, making a loud noise.

The sound was so loud that it carried all the way down to Mary's back bedroom. Mary was sitting-up in bed watching television. Mary called out.

"Jimmy, is that you? What are you doing up there?"

There was no answer, it was silent again. Mary accepted that it was Jimmy coming home early.

The two men walked into Jimmy's bedroom, turned the light on and began searching. The room was decorated with many antiques and gold and silver painted furniture. Numerous photos hung on the walls and set on his dresser of the places to which Jimmy had traveled, such as San Francisco, Hawaii, England, Ireland and Rome. On a pedestal in the corner of the room was Jimmy's treasured miniature white statue of David.

Taylor said, AJust a bunch of crap in here."

Sarlo opened a drawer. "The jewelry is mostly costume shit, not worth anything."

"Well, take it all, you never know some of it may be valuable. See if you can find some more cash," Taylor said. AI'm going downstairs to see what I can find." He walked down the stairs, through the hallway and into the kitchen, which was lit by a florescent light over the sink. He looked around the table and countertops for anything of value, but found nothing. Then Taylor walked into the dining room, which was used to house Mike's old butterfly collection. As Taylor walked past the open door of the rear bedroom, he was astonished to see that Mrs. Zappalorti was actually home and in bed watching television.

He darted back to the hall and went upstairs to warn Sarlo. Mary had definitely seen the shadowy figure of someone crossing her doorway, but she wasn't sure who it was. She lowered the volume on

160

the TV, then called out, "Jimmy, is that you? Jimmy!"

No one answered, so she slowly got out of bed and put her bathrobe and slippers on. Mary walked out into the dining room and turned the light on. The colorful wings of the mounted butterflies shimmered from the reflection of the light as she walked past. She slowly shuffled toward the kitchen and got her wooden rolling pin from the draw, just in case there was a prowler. Then she slowly walked back to the dining room and towards the living room.

Taylor returned to Jimmy's room, where Sarlo was still rifling the dresser drawers.

He nervously said, "Phil, the old lady's home. She saw me walk past her room." Sarlo replied, "Oh, shit! Let's get the fuck out of here before she gets a good look."

Taylor and Sarlo walked out into the hallway and looked downstairs. It was dark, no one was there. Both men quietly walked down the stairs. As they reached the bottom step, the hall light went on. Mary was standing in the living room doorway. When Mary saw the two strangers she knew something was very wrong. However, she did not know she was confronting her son's murderers.

Mary brandished her wooden rolling pin and demanded, "Who are you and what are you doing in my house?"

Sarlo stammered, "Oh, we're friends of your son. He asked us to get something from his room. He told us to meet him here."

Mary asked, "Well, how did you get in the house?"

Taylor replied, "He lent us his keys. We unlocked the door and came in. We didn't think anyone was home." Becoming very nervous and threatened by the old woman's boldness, he reached into his pocket for his knife. Sarlo knew what his partner was thinking and grabbed his hand. Sarlo took Jimmy's keys from his pocket and held them up for Mary to see.

Sarlo said, "We should just leave now." He went toward the front porch and stood with his back to the wall, by a bookcase.

Mary held-up the rolling pin and said, "Give me Jimmy's keys or

I'll bop you on the head."

Sarlo said, "Sure." He dropped the keys in her open hand.

Mary asked, "Where's Jimmy?"

Taylor stammered, "Ah, he's probably on his way. He told us to meet him here. Can I use your phone?"

Mary agreed he could make a call, and pointed to the phone on the end table in the living room. Taylor dialed a number and made a brief call, but Mary was distracted when she heard the front door swing open. She looked out into the hall at Sarlo, who just opened the door and was standing in the doorway.

Taylor returned from the living room and walked past Mary, to the front hallway. Sarlo saw Taylor begin to reach for his knife again.

"No, Mike, we got what we came for. Let's just leave now."

The two men quickly walked out the front door. Mary watched them suspiciously. She closed and locked the door behind them, breathing a sigh of relief that they were now outside.

Mary looked out the small window at the top of the front door. She could see Taylor and Sarlo standing at the curb talking.

Outside, Taylor said to Sarlo, "Why did you stop me from killing her? Now she can probably identify us."

Sarlo hissed, "You dumb fuck. It's bad enough you killed Jimmy. We were only supposed to kick the shit out of him. I'm not going to let you kill that old woman, too."

"Well if we get caught it's your fault," Taylor answered. AI should go back there and slit her throat! Then there are no witnesses. Dead people can't talk"

Sarlo said, "Mike, let's just get out of here while the getting's good. I'm not going back to jail for you or anyone else.

Taylor replied, "We should kill her. She knows what we look like. She can finger us, but let's go before the old man gets home."

Taylor then looked back at the Zappalorti house, reached into his pocket and took out his knife. Sarlo shook his head. Taylor put the knife back in his pocket. Quickly, they walked up Androvette Street and disappeared into the night.

When Mike arrived home at 10:45 P.M. from his meeting, Mary told him about the two men who had been in the house. He was shocked and angry. Mary told him that they said they were Jimmy's friends, but she had never met them before and thought that they were lying. She knew most of Jimmy's friends. Since it was too difficult for her to go up the hallway stairs due to her shortness of breath from emphysema, she did not know that they had broken open Jimmy's bedroom door or had stolen cash and jewelry. Mike was angry that someone had actually been in the house. Thinking they were his youngest son's friends, he was angry at Jimmy for giving them his keys.

Mike turned the hall light on and went up. When he got to the top of the stairs he shouted down to Mary, AHoly shit, they broke Jimmy's bedroom door open. His room's a mess. All his dresser draws are ransacked."

Mary stood at the bottom of the stairs looking up at Mike. Mike came out of Jimmy's bed room and looked down at his wife. "I'd better check my room. I have some cash in my end table draw."

Mary replied in disbelieve, "They robbed us, those scoundrels. I didn't know, Mike."

He walked into his room. "Son-of-a-bitch, they were in here too! All my draws are open, my hundred dollars is gone. They also took the Holy Eucharist case! I'm gonna call the cops." Mike went into the kitchen and dialed 911. A patrol car with two police officers from the 123rd Precinct arrived at the house fifteen minutes later. They carefully noted the damage, took a report on the burglary, and promised to send someone back in the morning to take fingerprints. Jimmy did not come home before Michael went to bed. He was very annoyed at him for allowing someone to come in the house with his keys. Michael still did not know his youngest son was floating in the Arthur Kill River.

Chapter 29 - Jimmy, Are You in Here?

MICHAEL ZAPPALORTI DID not sleep much during the night. He kept waiting to hear the sound of Jimmy coming in the front door and making noise the way he generally did. In the past Mike would get angry at Jimmy for waking him up from his sleep, but not that night. On Tuesday morning, January 23rd, 1990, at 7:30 AM, Michael shook Mary awake in her downstairs bedroom.

"Mary, Mary, wake up! Jimmy never came home last night. His bed wasn't slept in."

Mary opened her eyes. "I'm worried, Mike. You better call Mickey and let him know."

A few minutes later, Mickey pulled up in front of the shop to begin work in the glass studio.

He got out of his truck, walked to the shop entrance, and unlocked the door. He went to the desk and began the habits of his day, checking his answering machine for messages. He activated the tape, listened and wrote down a phone number.

Mike, Sr. entered from the side door. He launched into the bizarre happenings of the previous night and the fact that Jimmy had not come home.

"Is Mom awake?" Mickey asked. "I want to talk to her."

AYes. I just made her coffee," Mike said. "Come in and have cup with us."

Mickey went upstairs to inspect the damage to Jimmy's door and look around, then went back down to speak with his mother. As soon as Mary saw her oldest son, she asked, AMickey, would you please walk down to Jimmy's shack and see if he's there?"

Mickey tried to disguise his great concern. "I'll go right now."

Mickey crossed Androvette Street and walked down the dirt road at the edge of next door neighbor Owen Reiter's property. He swiftly made his way through the giant reeds and willow trees that shimmered gently in the cool January morning breeze. Gray skies loomed overhead as he followed the road towards Jimmy's shack. As he approached, he noticed many footprints, a large reddish stain in the center of the path, and a drag mark. He knelt and examined the red substance in the sand. Then put the tip of his right index finger into it.

He rubbed his fingers together and realized it was blood.

He stood up and called out, "Jimmy, Jimmy, you here?"

Receiving no reply, he quickly ran toward the cabin. The front door was ajar. He pushed it all the way open and went inside. He looked around the kitchen, then in the bedroom to make sure Jimmy wasn't sleeping.

The beach house was deserted. It looked as though the place had been ransacked. He went back into the front room and called again in vain for his brother. He walked out the door and stood at the edge of the sand path. From his vantage point he could now see distinct footprints, a blood trail and drag marks in the sand. They led down to the beach.

Mickey ran to the steps that led to the beach. As he walked down the steps he spotted his younger brother lying near the dock at the water's edge. He was on his back in the sand, clad only in his underwear. The many knife cuts and punctures in his lifeless body were all too visible.

Crying out in agony, Mickey ran to his brother's side. He knelt and touched Jimmy's shoulder, hoping against hope that Jimmy was alive. The flesh was cold and clammy. He slowly placed his hand on his brother's forehead and caressed him for a moment. Then he stood up and screamed into the sky, "No…no…they killed my brother!!!!"

Mickey's voice echoed across the Arthur Kill River. In shock, he plodded slowly to the stairs and collapsed into a sitting position. He looked again at his brother's body, put his face into his cupped hands, and began to sob uncontrollably.

After a time, Mickey regained his composure, knowing he had to calm and collect himself to tell his parents their youngest son was dead. On the way back, he avoided the blood-stained sand. He did not want to disturb the crime scene. With resignation, head down, he walked lead-footed toward the glass shop and his parent's home. When he got back to the shop, he dialed 911 and reported that his brother was murdered.

Mickey lingered a few minutes while he gathered his thoughts and regained his composure. He then went into the house. He wanted to tell his father at first in the privacy of the shop, needing to protect his mother from the bad news. But as he entered the house from the side door, he found Mary and Mike sitting at the kitchen table. When they saw the sad expression on Mickey's face, both Mary and Mike immediately asked if Jimmy was all right. Mickey paused for a moment, "No, he's not all right. They killed him. He's dead."

The house filled with screams of disbelief. Mike Senior wanted to go see his son, but Mickey prevented him. Instead, they hugged, cried, and prayed for Jimmy's soul while they waited for the police to arrive.

The following week, when interviewed by Dr. Patrick J. Suraci (a New York psychologist and professional counselor who came to help the family cope with Jimmy's death), Michael Zappalorti, Jr. recalled that dreadful day. "There was so much blood. It looked like a slaughter house. I knew he had to be dead. The blood was all in a big circle on the path, and then a trail all the way down to the edge of the beach. He was behind the dock, not far from a row boat, just laying there in the sand. He only had his underwear on. After discovering Jimmy's body, I went to the stained glass studio and called 911. After doing that, I knew it was time to tell my mother and father the horrible news. The detectives said the murderers stabbed him several times in the chest and cut his throat. I hope he didn't linger too long. I had thoughts in my mind that he was still alive when they threw him in the water. The memory haunts me. It's going to take me a long time to get it out of my head. I saw stuff when I was in the service, I always thought I was tough. But it's different when it's your own. I just wish I could get over it. Thank God, it rained two days after the murder. It washed most of his blood away."

Mickey then began making the dreaded calls to reach his sister Peggy and brother Bob. Mickey called his wife Carol, who comforted her husband and offered to call Peggy for him.

Peggy recalled, "Mickey's wife Carol called me at work. She was very upset and told me what happened. I became hysterical. I just couldn't believe it. That was the beginning of the nightmare. I called my daughter Elizabeth and told her what happened. When I arrived home, my daughter Betsy was waiting for me. She drove me from my home in New Jersey to my parents' house on Staten Island."

Chapter 30 - I'm Sorry for Your Loss

WITHIN AN HOUR of Mickey calling 911, Jimmy's shack and the entire surrounding area was swarmed by police and news reporters. Assigned to the murder investigation were two plainclothes police detectives from the 122nd Precinct Homicide Squad, Robert Bergin and Larry Jensen. They were taking notes while questioning Michael Zappalorti, Jr. Mickey was understandably agitated by all the media and constant questions. Police photographers captured gruesome images of Jimmy lying on shore near the dock. A uniformed policeman, Officer Ellington, interrupted the chaos of sounds. "Was the coroner called? Dammit, somebody get on the horn to the Medical Examiner!"

A second uniformed policeman, Officer Halleran, repeatedly called out in vain for witnesses.

A third uniformed policeman, Officer Gross, was on the phone with the Medical Examiner. "I'd say about ten hours, maybe twelve. Yeah, cut from ear to ear. That's right. Around 8:30 last night, yeah."

Other police officers cordoned the area with yellow crime scene tape. An ambulance was parked several feet away from the path that fed down to the beach. Two medics took notes and talked to somebody on the ambulance radio. Another New York City police car pulled up and a policeman named Harvey got out and headed toward a group of police officers who were in conference.

Officer Harvey asked, "Who's in charge? I have Monsignor Finn here from St. Joseph - St. Thomas Parish, to give the victim the last rites." Detectives Bergin and Jensen answered almost simultaneously and directed the pair down toward the beach.

Monsignor Finn replied, 'The Zappalorti family called me to give their son the last rites." More newspaper reporters pulled up in their vans with remote satellite dishes mounted on the roofs to cover the scene. Television news teams tried to conduct interviews with the police. One of the TV reporters interrupted Mickey by shoving a microphone in his face.

"Did your brother have any enemies, Mr. Zappalorti?"

Mickey stared at her for a moment, then walked away. Monsignor Finn was led down to where a forensic detective named Carter carefully measured the body and how far it lay from the small wooden dock. A policeman stood behind him taping off areas where the ground has been disturbed. Monsignor Finn noted that a Saint Christopher's medal hung around Jimmy's neck.

Officer Gross shouted, "Hey, Carter! Detective Jensen wants you up here to take a look at something."

"What?"

"Never mind what; just get your ass up here."

"All right, I'm comin', I'm comin'."

Monsignor Finn was left by himself next to Jimmy's body. Slowly, he took out his white- and-gold-banded stole and kissed it. He placed the stole around his neck and knelt and looked down at Jimmy. Monsignor Finn observed the gold crucifix ring on Jimmy's finger. He had seen Jimmy's ring before when he attended mass. Monsignor Finn began the prayer for the departed while he made the sign of the Lord with his thumb in the center of Jimmy's forehead.

After completing his prayers, Monsignor Finn stood and removed his stole. He noticed drops of blood on it from when he touched Jimmy. Monsignor Finn saw Mickey, who stood on the bottom step of the stairs leading to the beach. They said hello and then Monsignor Finn asked, "Mike, how old was your brother?"

"Just forty-four," Mickey answered.

"He was that old, I thought he was younger, I'm sorry for your loss," Monsignor Finn said.

Detective Bergin appeared, "Father, are you finished here, we have to remove the body."

"Yes detective, I'm done," Monsignor Finn said.

While walking, Bergin asked, "What parish you with, Father?"

"St. Joseph - St. Thomas Parish, from this area of Staten Island. I knew the victim and his entire family. Jimmy's father, Michael is a Deacon in my Parish," Monsignor Finn said.

"I'm finished here now, so could Officer Harvey drive me back to the Zappalorti home where I left my car?"

"Sure Father. He'll take you right away," Detective Bergin said.

Mickey stood near the two detectives as they looked at the murder scene. Detectives Bergin and Jensen were examining two sets of shoe prints, side by side.

"Look here, Michael, bare footprints. Those are your brother's. He was probably killed on this spot. See the pool of blood on the path," Bergin asked?

"I know exactly where all the blood is, I was the first one here," Mickey said.

Yeah, I know, but we have to go over this stuff," Jensen said.

Detective Bergin continued, "Then you can see drag marks and drops of blood leading to the beach. We'll make casts of the prints, but I tell you one of these guys was wearing a size twelve. He probably did the knifing. The other guy's prints look about size ten. The bigger guy was wearing boots. The size ten guy was in sneakers."

Mickey nodded in agreement.

"The two suspects mull around here, while the body print and blood are here. Looks like they're wondering what to do with him. Then they pick him up and drag him to the beach."

The policemen followed the clues to the edge of the sandy path to the beach. Mickey lit a cigarette and slowly trailed behind them.

When they arrived on the beach Detective Jensen continued his analysis of the crime scene.

"They threw him in the water here. Probably thought the tide would take him out to sea. They screwed up."

"Vicious bastards, what could have been their motive," Mickey asked?

"Drugs? Behind in his payments? Argument over money," Detective Bergin theorized. "We'll figure it out."

Hearing that, Mickey exploded, "What the fuck are you talking about! My brother didn't use or sell drugs. That's bullshit."

Just then, Police Officer Matt Metoosak came down the stairs and called out, "Detective Bergin, I found a wallet!"

As Metoosak handed the wallet to Bergin, a crowd gathered. Bergin opened the wallet and looked through it. He pulled out some business cards and a photograph.

Detective Jensen asked, "What do you make of it, Bob?"

"Twenty six dollars in cash. A Navy I.D. card. Hmm, no driver's license. That's it. A picture of an older woman and man. Mike, is this your brother's?"

He passed the wallet to Mickey, who confirmed the facts. He pulled out some business cards, some of which were Michael and Sons Stained Glass. Before any of them could comment, two medics and Officer Gross come down the stairs onto the beach to remove Jimmy's body. The policeman laid a black body bag next to Jimmy and unzipped it.

The gruesome business was too much for Mickey. He told the detectives, "I've had enough. I'm going home to be with my family while you guys do your jobs."

After Mickey left, the detectives continued to work the crime scene. Two officers helped the medics lift Jimmy's body into the ambulance. It would be taken to the Richmond County Medical Examiner's laboratory for autopsy.

Chapter 31 - Two Fatal Wounds

SEVERAL HOURS AFTER Jimmy was murdered, his body was at the Richmond County Medical Examiner's laboratory for an autopsy. Detectives Bergin and Jensen came to witness the completion of the physical examination. Jimmy was stretched out on the examination table while the Medical Examiner was finalizing the stitching of the body cavity.

A microphone was suspended over the table, and the medical examiner spoke into it every once in awhile. He was a middle aged man, brown hair turning gray on the sides, had a stout, round, clean-shaven face with eyeglasses hanging from the tip of his nose. He paused from his examination.

"So, what's your interest in this man, detectives?"

"We wanted to know how many times he was stabbed for one thing," Detective Jensen said.

The Medical Examiner delivered his final comments into the microphone.

"Death was a result of repeated punctures with a sharp-bladed instrument. It was most likely a non-serrated, five-inch knife. There are two fatal wounds. One administered across the juggler vein and the other punctured the right lung causing death within minutes,"

The Medical Examiner turned off the microphone and said, "He was stabbed eight times in addition to his throat being cut."

At last, Detective Bergin felt able to speak. "When you run your laboratory tests, I'd like to know if this man had any drugs in his system. Hard ones?"

"Sure, Detective, I'll let you know if we find any evidence of drugs. I can tell you this: He was a smoker and a drinker. You can smell beer on his breath, and look at the nicotine stains on his fingers."

Both detectives shook their heads in agreement while looking at Jimmy's body. Aside from the fresh stitches from the M.E. closing the autopsy wounds, Detective Bergin noticed a rather large old scar across the lower stomach area of the body.

"What would cause such a large scar like this, Doc," Detective Bergin asked?

That's an old surgical scar, detective. It's associated with major surgery due to serious infection of the lower rectal canal. For instance, if a patient had inflammation or a puncture to the peritoneum, it would require massive doses of Penicillin to fight the infection. Or in this case, I suspect Jimmy had peritonitis that required surgery to save his life.

"How would someone get their peritoneum ruptured," Detective Jensen asked?

The M.E. explained, "This man had forced trauma in the anus. But based upon the amount of scaring on the rectal canal wall, I'd say someone shoved an elongated object forcefully up his ass, which caused that amount of damage."

"You mean he was raped with a broom handle," Detective Bergin asked?

"Frankly, yes. Some elongated object was forced into his anus, all the way up to where the rectal canal turns sharply. The object penetrated the peritoneum, caused leakage of fecal matter into the body cavity, and thus the need for surgery.

"Jesus Christ, that must have been painful," Detective Jensen said.

"It probably was. If not treated quickly, it could have caused death," the M.E. informed.

"Larry, I wonder if there is any record of the incident in the police data base," Detective Bergin said. He made some notes in his log book. "We'll check our files, or we can ask his parents if they have any details about what happened when we go there later."

Detectives Bergin and Jensen started to leave. Detective Jensen, stopped and turned back to the medical examiner.

"One more thing. When you send your report, could you tell me what his alcohol blood content was? Just curious if he was drunk when he was murdered."

Detectives Bergin and Jensen thanked the M. E., and went out the door. As soon they went outside, they both lit cigarettes. As they walked towards their unmarked squad car, Detective Bergin said, "What time is it? We better get over to the Zappalorti home to interview the family."

"It's almost two in the morning. Let's get over there now," Detective Jensen replied.

Chapter 32 - The Family Gathering

AT 12:36 P.M., on January 24, 1990, the neighborhood around the Zappalorti house was cluttered with parked cars in front of the two story wood frame house. Robert parked his car among the other vehicles on Androvette Street and approached his family's house. He walked lead-footed up the four cement steps and through the front door, which stood wide open. Inside the home, the living room was packed with people. His father paced around the room, working off the excess energy of frustration and anger. His mother appeared calm, her mental state bolstered by her family. Next to her was her only daughter, Peggy and Peggy's husband, Richard Marlow. Peggy's daughters, Elizabeth and Suzette and Peggy's son-in-law, Andy Sutton were seated along the wall.

Robert's four children, Debbie, Kelly, Robert Jr. and Michael were also there. Don Shepler, Jimmy's long-time companion and friend sat on a folding chair along the living room wall, near Mary.

Greetings were given, emotions expressed, and the same sentences of confusion were repeated yet again.

"Do the police have any idea who did this?" Robert asked.

Peggy related the break-in of the house and the confrontation with Mary. She had already given brief descriptions. Mary said, "This morning two homicide detectives were here. They said they would be back this evening to interview me and your father."

Robert set to writing an obituary, the melancholy task to

summarizing an entire life. Prominent in the article was Jimmy's passion for music and that he loved art in general and making stained glass windows with his father and brother in specific.

The gathering waited for Detectives Bergin and Jensen, who were scheduled to interview Mary around eight o'clock. They prayed together and reminisced. Michael, Sr. said, "Jimmy seemed to always have bad luck."

"Even on the day he was born we had trouble," Mary agreed. "He almost didn't make it into this world. As an adult they tried to kill him in Vietnam, he was hit by a cab in Rome, and in New York City they beat him up, raped him and mugged him in the bars, subway and streets. But my Jimmy survived it all! Who'd of thought he'd end- p getting killed right here in his own backyard?"

Robert's oldest daughter, Debbie Mournet asked, "What do you mean, Nana? Why wasn't he almost born?"

Mary continued, "We lived in Brooklyn, on Third Avenue, at the time. I was at the end of my ninth month of pregnancy. He was born in late summer, on September 29, 1945. I hemorrhaged and almost had a miscarriage. The doctor said the bleeding was caused by too much pressure from such a large baby. Jimmy was 9 pounds. The doctor also thought I overdid it by working too much in the glass store and around the house. He was born by Caesarean section, I remember your grandfather proudly saying, 'Hello, son. Welcome to the Zappalorti family,' I think it was my faith in God that helped me through almost losing Jimmy before he was born. I thought about what Saint Thomas Aquinas said in the summa, 'We do not believe to know, we try to know in order to believe.' That's what makes us Catholics different from many other Christian faiths."

Chapter 33 - The Police Detectives Arrive

OUT OF THEIR collective sorrow, the Zappalorti family and friends wove a new-found closeness as they all sat in conversation in the comfort of the living room. The peaceful mood was broken when the front doorbell rang. It was close to 02:30 A.M.

Richard Marlow got up. "I'll get it Mike, you stay seated."

A minute later, Richard and the two detectives came into the living room. Detectives Larry Bergin and Robert Jensen were seasoned detectives and knew how to find criminals. Although Jensen and Bergin looked like businessmen in their suits, they were in fact street-smart cops. After the formalities, the two detectives explained what evidence was found at the crime scene and the results of their interviews with people in the neighborhood. Then they began the painstaking process of pulling every possible detail from Mike and Mary about what transpired when the intruders came into the house the night before.

Everyone's eyes were glued on Mary and Michael talking with the detectives. Detective Jensen was asking questions, while Detective Bergin stood quietly in a corner and listened. He noted a large wooden crucifix hung on the white wall behind Mary.

Detective Jensen noted, "Mr. Zappalorti, why weren't you home last night?"

"I was at the Al-Anon meeting, like I told you before, I was sponsoring a new member."

"Did Jimmy have a drinking problem? Was he a member of AA?"

"Jimmy drank beer and wine, mostly on weekends," Robert answered.

"Sometimes with his friends," Michael added.

"Yeah, but sometimes too much," Mary volunteered.

"Jimmy drank to blow off steam, that's all," Michael said.

"Maybe the two guys who confronted you last night were his drinking buddies," Detective Jensen suggested.

"Believe me, they weren't his friends," Mary said confidently. "I never saw the likes of those men before last night."

"You sure you knew all his friends," Detective Jensen asked?

"No, of course not," Mary said. I know Don here and their buddy, Lou. The two men in my house last night were rough, rude and unsophisticated – not like Jimmy's friends," Mary said with assurance.

"How do you know, Mom," Mickey said? "You never met all of Jimmy's queer friends."

At the mention of the word "queer," the two detectives were reminded to ask about Jimmy being raped. Until that moment, no one had given any indication that Jimmy was a gay man.

Detectives Bergin asked, "How long have you known your son was gay?"

Mary told about Jimmy's experience in Vietnam, and his gay affair with another sailor. About the way they were beaten and how Jimmy had been almost murdered. When he was discharged from the Navy, that was the first hard clue the family gained about Jimmy's homosexuality. Peggy walked to the piano, took the formal Navy photograph of Jimmy, and gave it to Detective Bergin. "Jimmy being gay, it surprised all of us," Peggy said.

"Mrs. Zappalorti, could you tell us if one of the men was wearing biker's boots?" Detective Bergin asked

"I never looked down at their feet," Mary said. "I was watching their faces. That's how I knew they were lying."

"Were they wearing leather or chains?"

"Now that you mention it, the one with the beard had a leather jacket with chains," Mary recalled.

"Maybe they were from the Ramrod Club," Robert suggested. For a time, the discussion revolved around the Ramrod, a rough place in the Village, where a number of violent men hung out.

"Was Jimmy a regular there?" Detective Jensen asked.

"Jimmy liked to dress in leather once in awhile. He'd go to the Ramrod sometimes," Robert said. "He liked role playing and watching what went on, but he mostly liked listening to the live music. He played piano at The Pink Flamingo bar."

"You don't understand, detectives," Mary tried to explain. "Anyone who really knew Jimmy was not threatened by him. They wouldn't want to hurt Jimmy. He was, how can I say it...?

"Innocent," Robert blurted out.

Everybody in the room turned and looked at Robert, Sr.

"Yes. That's it," Mary said. "That's the word I was looking for."

"Was Jimmy well liked, Mrs. Zappalorti," asked Detective Jensen?

"Yes he was," Mary acknowledged. "Everyone who knew him loved him."

"Do you think he kept secrets from you, Mrs. Zappalorti?" Detective Jensen asked.

"Why, yes. Even when he was a little boy, we never knew what he was thinking. He would collect things and keep them in secret places. I'd find coins and toys hidden in his dresser draws. He would pick up pieces of colored glass and save them in a cigar box."

"May I see more of Jimmy's photos," asked Detective Jensen?

Peggy collected a few more photos of Jimmy and handed them to the detectives.

"I have a question for you, Detective Bergin," Michael said. "Have you found out if anyone has been harassing Jimmy around Charleston?"

Detective Bergin replied, "What I can tell you, based upon all the interviews we did in the neighborhood, is that on Monday afternoon, at about 3:30 P.M., two men started harassing Jimmy as he left the Deli Delight, up the block. The two men were yelling at Jimmy. The store clerk, a Ms. Tawil, reported this."

Mary was gently but insistently interrogated, asked the same questions six different ways, until she finally broke down. The detectives understood the limits.

"You've been all very helpful," Detective Jensen said, rising from his chair. "We'll get these punks. Maybe Mrs. Zappalorti can identify these guys from the mug books."

And we'll have to send over the forensics' guys to lift prints," Detective Bergin added. "We might get lucky. Everybody in the house will have to give us prints."

"The kids too," Peggy asked?

Detectives Jensen and Begin both nod, yes. "We'll be in contact about when we return with the mug books," Detective Jensen said.

The two detectives said their goodbyes, and left the Zappalorti home.

Before everyone began dispersing for home, Mary suggested a group prayer.

Detectives Bergin and Jensen stopped outside the Zappalorti home to light cigarettes. They noticed the glass studio and tried the front door. It was open, so they went inside to look around. There was a dim night light on the workshop table. Bergin turned the overhead florescent light on. It threw a ghostly soft light around the workshop. On the work benches he saw beautiful stained glass windows in various stages of completion. All the windows depict various religious scenes. The two detectives admired the quality of the workmanship, the fine detail, and most of all the way the different pieces of colored glass had been cut. Jensen picked up a hand- painted face of Saint Peter and held it to the light.

"We thought you went home," Mickey said.

Detectives Bergin and Jensen were startled at the sound of a voice. They turned around and saw Mickey and Robert standing in the doorway.

"We were curious and wanted to see where Jimmy worked," Detective Jensen answered.

"We need to lock up," Robert said. "We're all exhausted. You're welcome to come back another time during the day to see the studio if you wish."

"Oh sure, we understand." They slowly walked past the two Zappalorti brothers. Mickey locked the door behind him.

Chapter 34 - I'll Speak at Jimmy's Funeral

ON JANUARY 24, 1990, at 09:30 A.M., the phone rang at the office of the New York Catholic Archdiocese. Sitting in the outer office was Monsignor Brian Coheran, Cardinal O'Connor's assistant and secretary. Monsignor Coheran answered the phone, "Cardinal O'Connor's office. How may I help you?"

"Yeah, this is Owen Reiter calling. The reason for my call is I'm requesting if Cardinal O'Connor would come to give a sermon at a funeral mass for my neighbors' son, James Zappalorti? He was murdered two days ago behind my house here on Staten Island," Owen said.

Monsignor Coheran said cautiously with his Irish accent, "Well sir, the Cardinal does not normally give sermons at funerals unless the deceased is a Catholic dignitary, a politician, or personal friend."

Owen Reiter explained, "Well, the Zappalorti family are devout Catholics. Mr. Zappalorti, senior is a Deacon at St. Joseph - St. Thomas Parish, here on Staten Island. The family is close friends with Monsignor Peter Finn, the Pastor of the church. Mrs. Zappalorti's sister is a nun in the Order of the Sisters of Charity, and the family makes stained glass windows for churches all over the northeastern United States."

While listening to Owen Reiter about the Zappalorti family, Monsignor Coheran happens to look at the headlines of the *New York Daily News* and the *New York Post*, lying on the corner of his desk. The *Daily News* headline was "Rage over Staten Island Slaying, "with a photo under the headline of Jimmy Zappalorti playing the piano. The headline of the *Post* blared "Staten Island Murder – an Act of Hate," with a photo of Jimmy in his Navy uniform.

Monsignor Coheran said with his Irish accent, "Can you give me your phone number, Mr. Reiter? I'll be explaining this to his Eminence to see if he will consider your request."

After giving him his phone number, Owen Reiter said, "Please do whatever you can. The Zappalorti family will be very grateful if the Cardinal could come. Thanks and good bye."

Monsignor Coheran started reading the newspaper stories in detail and made some notes about the unusual circumstances. He punched in some numbers on the telephone pad.

"Your Eminence," Monsignor Coheran said. "Thought you should know that I just received a phone call from a Mr. Owen Reiter on Staten Island. The family of the man that was murdered yesterday wants you to attend the funeral. Yes, that's right. Okay, I'll be right in."

Monsignor Coheran picked up the two newspapers from his desk and walked toward the huge polished double oak doors at the end of the antechamber. He knocked and stepped through the doorway and entered Cardinal O'Connor's office.

Cardinal O'Connor said, "I've read the newspaper articles on the story as well. Indeed it's an unfortunate event that the young man was murdered, but I have no connection with the family. You know the man was a homosexual. A homosexual!"

"The victim was forty-four years old," Monsignor Coheran informed.

"A middle-aged homosexual," Cardinal O'Connor corrected. "The news media and papers are going to turn this whole thing into a Catholic vendetta. That's exactly what we don't want."

"He was a Catholic," Monsignor Coheran interrupted. "His father's a deacon at St. Joseph - St. Thomas Parish. His aunt was a

Catholic nun in the Order of the Sisters of Charity and the family makes stained glass windows for churches all over the northeastern United States."

Surprised about the new information that was not in the newspapers, O'Connor's demeanor changed. He looked up at Brian and said, "Please get me the family's phone number. I'd like to speak with the victim's father."

Cardinal O'Connor's face showed deep concern as he sat there thinking. "I probably should speak at Jimmy Zappalorti's funeral. Especially if the family members are devote Catholics. However, the point is to embrace the soul, but not the sin. I must inform the congregation at the funeral what the scriptures tell us to do."

Cardinal O'Connor asked, "What was the name of the man who called here this morning?"

"His name was Owen Reiter, your Eminence," Monsignor Coheran said.

"Call him back and tell him I'll speak at Jimmy Zappalorti's funeral. Make all the arrangements with the Pastor of St. Joseph's Church," Cardinal O'Connor said.

"Brian, I want to issue a press release. It must deliver a harsh condemnation of the murder of the Staten Island gay man. Have it say that if a person perpetrates violence, in any form against a homosexual, they do an evil thing. Whatever they may pretend to be, they are not Christians. Anyone who thinks church condemnation of 'homosexual behavior' means it's all right to attack gays is grossly ignorant."

Because of his outspokenness about homosexuality, Cardinal O'Connor was often targeted by gay rights groups who led several demonstrations against him. Holy Masses officiated by Cardinal O'Connor were sometimes interrupted by gay rights activists and protestors who chained themselves to pews and disrupted services. In one case, a gay pride parade was deliberately routed in front of St. Patrick's Cathedral. But in the protester's defense, Cardinal O'Connor urged the congregation: "Please do not believe for a moment that you would be defending the Church or advancing Church teachings by expressions of hatred."

Chapter 35 - Justice for Jimmy!

GATHERED IN FRONT of Gracie Mansion, the office and home of the New York City mayor, were about one hundred and fifty protestors. Most were gay men and lesbians carrying signs. The sign messages included: Pass the Bill, End Hate Crimes; Gays Have Rights Too; We're Not Going Back in the Closet, and Justice for Jimmy Zappalorti. A collection of newspaper and TV reporters took pictures and notes. Matt Forman, the Executive Director of the New York City Gay and Lesbian Anti-Violence Project, stood on the back of a decorated flatbed truck. He held an electronic bullhorn and is a cheerleader for the crowd of protesters. Yelling into the bullhorn, Matt Foreman said, "We want justice for Jimmy Zappalorti. We want the Mayor out here! Where is Mayor Dinkins? Where is Mayor Dinkins? Dinkins! Dinkins!"

The entire crowd took up the chant. Matt yelled, "Justice for Jimmy! Justice for Jimmy!" The protestors repeated the demand.

Across from City Park stood dozens of New York City Police officers, in riot gear and on horseback. They awaited orders from the Police Commissioner to move between the group of protestors and Gracie Mansion.

Anyone who gets to be mayor of New York City is by definition extremely savvy politically. David Dinkins was of that ilk. In the main hallway of Gracie Mansion, Mayor Dinkins hurried into his main meeting room, pulling along a wake of staffers. The staffers handed him newspaper clippings, e-mail messages, and police file folders. They throw open the doors to the meeting room and all go inside. The crowd's roars penetrated the large windows... They gathered down around a huge polished table which had several phones on it.

Dinkins had already given the situation considerable thought. He informed the group that they needed to get on the right side of this homosexual murder issue. A press release needed to be drafted ASAP, expressing Dinkins' anger and frustration over Albany's lack of action in passing hate crimes legislation against minorities. He wanted specific mention of blacks and gays as hate crime targets. The murder of James Zappalorti was to be the tinder that finally lit the fire.

Another assistant was directed to contact the Police Commissioner and emphasize how anxious Dinkins' office was to bring the murderers to justice. In addition, the Mayor wanted to know where the funeral for Zappalorti would be held and whether or not his family would mind if he showed up at the church to pay his respects.

A suggestion was made to promote a reward for information leading to an arrest.

"Good suggestion. Make it five thousand," Mayor Dinkins said. When he heard the New York City Gay and Lesbian Anti-Violence Project had already put up a five thousand dollar reward Dinkins' decided to raise the City's reward to ten thousand.

"Now, let's disarm this protest. Go out there and tell their leader I want a meeting with him. Ask him to bring a few of his staffers. Then schedule a press conference in two hours. Make sure Governor Cuomo, Senator Paterson, Ruth Messenger and Rudy Giuliani are all invited. This homosexual murder could have both state and federal implications."

Outside Gracie Mansion the screaming continued: "Justice for Jimmy! Justice for Jimmy Zappalorti!"

Chapter 36 - The Victim in Every Case

THE FOLLOWING DAY, Detectives Bergin and Jensen walked into the 122nd Precinct, located on Hylan Boulevard, in Staten Island. It was late morning, with a January chill in the windy air. Detective Bergin carried a thick manila file folder under his arm. The uniformed sergeant at the front desk tipped his hat as they walked past. In the squad room, there were other detectives and uniformed police officers at desks working on typewriters, filling out the onerous forms associated with arrests and general police work. The detectives stopped at an office door with the lettered words, Computer Data Center.

The office was kept neat and had several work stations. Only one police officer was busy at a work stations entering criminal records into the data base. He nodded hello to the detectives. An ashtray was half filled with butts. There were pictures on the wall of the Precinct boxing, softball and bowling teams. Detective Bergin sat down at one of the computers and Jensen stood behind him. Detective Bergin became engrossed with something on the computer screen. Without looking up, he said, "Larry, you got your notes on the Zappalorti autopsy?"

The Medical Examiner said he had been dead for 12-hours. He was stabbed eight times and his throat was deeply cut," Detective Jensen informed.

Looking at his computer, Detective Bergin made the data entries

"Damn these things. I'm still learning how to use the search engine."

Detective Jensen reached over and punched the key pad, showing his partner a quick tutorial.

"How in the hell did you do that?" Detective Bergin asked.

Jokingly, Detective Jensen said, "I'm a magician."

Detective Jensen responded, "Yeah, magicians can do anything, right? I was wondering if James Zappalorti had a criminal record."

"What're you looking for felony arrests? Vice? Drugs?"

"Anything, I'd like to know more about him," Detective Bergin said. "They tell me with this computer you can bring up every arrest file in the five boroughs of New York for the past twenty years."

"You can, just type his name in the search field and enter 'History'," Detective Jensen directed.

"Wow, look at that! How many times was this guy mugged, robbed and beaten up? What's this, he was raped at the Ramrod," Detective Bergin said.

"That explains how his peritoneum got ruptured. Looks like Jimmy's been around the block," Detective Jensen said.

"But Larry, he's had no felony arrests. Jimmy just has a few drunk and disorderly tickets himself. Jesus, it looks like he's been the victim in every case. We should print a copy of this."

"Just hit the 'print' button," Detective Jensen said.

Detective Bergin clicks on print button and the computer printer goes to work. Jensen pulled the pages from the printer as they came out.

Detective Bergin said, "Hand me the files. I want to read some details of Jimmy's rape at the Ramrod."

"Okay, in the meantime I'm going to get the Mug Books I asked Sergeant Martindale to compile for us. After that we're done here," Jensen said.

As they walked through the precinct, Jensen retrieved the business card he had been given by Michael Zappalorti, Sr. He stopped at a desk and dialed the number.

"Zappalorti residence, who's calling," Mike asked?

"It's Detective Jensen, Mike. We'd like to come by with the Mug Books to show Mrs. Zappalorti."

"What time will you be arriving," Michael asked?

Detective Jensen informed. "We're at the 122nd Precinct now. We're ready to go, so we can be there in about a half hour."

"Sounds good, detective. See you then," Michael Zappalorti said.

Detective Jensen hung up the phone and looked to see where his partner was.

Detective Bergin came out of the squad room, then folded Jimmy's police report records carefully and placed them in his coat lapel pocket. The two detectives exited the building with purpose. They went to their squad car and drove south on Hylan Boulevard towards Charleston.

Chapter 37 - See Anybody Familiar, Mary?

BASED UPON THE results of fingerprint tests found at the crime scene and at the Zappalorti house, using the computer Detectives Bergin and Jensen narrowed down a series of mug shots from the photo library at the 122nd Precinct. The mug shots include a few individuals who are high on their list of suspects. When they arrived at the Zappalorti residence Mary was resting in her bedroom with Peggy and Mike sitting next to her. Mickey was out setting stained glass windows with Jim Anderson at a church in Brooklyn. The time was 1:00 P.M. Robert escorted the two detectives to Mary's bedroom. Blacky, the Labrador retriever barked loudly at the strangers and had to be calmed.

Detective Bergin began, "We got a hunch that maybe the guys who murdered your son were looking for a gay person to harass. It was just a hunch."

Mary puts on her eyeglasses and begins to look through the pages of mug shots. "They all look so mean," she remarked.

"Mrs. Zappalorti, our computer system gave us just the pictures of well known gang members, skin heads and gay-bashers from the five boroughs," Detective Jensen said. "They all have criminal records."

"See anybody familiar, Mary?" Michael asked.

"No, I don't recognize any of these men," Mary said after looking at each page carefully. She closed the first mug book.

196

Detective Jensen picked up the other book and handed it to her.

"I think one of them was wearing a sloppy beard, you know?" Mary said. "And his hair was messy...wait a minute! I think I found a picture of one of them, Detective Jensen!" She pointed to the photo.

Jensen smiled and nodded to his partner. "Bingo! She picked Sarlo."

Several pages later, she exclaimed, "My God! I'm looking at the other monster that killed our Jimmy!"

"You picked Michael Taylor. That was our hunch," Detective Bergin said. "May I use your phone Mr. Zappalorti?"

Mike pointed the direction. "Yes, go right ahead. Use the phone in the kitchen."

Detective Bergin exited the bedroom.

"We thought these might be the two guys," Detective Jensen said. "We'll get 'em."

"What gave you the hunch?" Peggy asked.

"Back in 1986, these two guys kidnapped a gay man in South Beach, Staten Island. They beat him with a tire iron, and then locked him in the trunk of his car. Sarlo and Taylor were deciding whether to set fire to the vehicle, threatening to blow it up or to drive it into the Atlantic Ocean to drown the man inside when a woman heard them arguing from her house and called the police. They were both arrested at the crime scene. They weren't charged with a bias crime, because the existing law didn't protect homosexuals. Even though their crime involved kidnapping, assault, and attempted murder, Taylor and Sarlo plea-bargained to attempted robbery. Taylor was charged as a juvenile and only served a year and a half. Sarlo served three years and was paroled in March of 1989."

"It's an outrage!" Peggy fumed. "If they were properly charged back in '86, they would still be in jail, and my brother would be alive."

"You're right," Detective Jensen said. "The victim didn't press charges because he didn't want to be exposed as a homosexual. We just arrest 'em; we don't sentence 'em! That's the job of the prosecutor and the judge."

"How fast can you nail the bastards?" Mike wanted to know.

Detective Bergin returned from the kitchen after making his phone calls.

"We may be able to get Taylor pretty fast; he lives in your neighborhood," Detective Jensen said.

Bergin looked crestfallen. "One lives right on Androvette Street. Just three houses up from you."

Michael slammed his fist into the nearest wall, knocking down a butterfly picture which shatters on the floor. He was in favor of marching to the house and dealing vigilante justice, but the detectives and the others in the room reasoned him to let the police do their jobs. Mike turned to his wife. "Go on, Mary. "You know what needs to be said."

Mary bowed her head. "Blessed art Thou, our Lord, our God who gave his only begotten Son to save us from eternal damnation. Forgive us our thoughts of revenge. We trust in Your protection. Please protect these brave police detectives as they pursue the murderers of our beloved son. Amen."

As the detectives were leaving, the next door neighbor, Owen Reiter, walked in to visit with the family. "Mary," Owen said, "I have some good news about the funeral mass for Jimmy. I called the Catholic Archdiocese of New York and told them how faithful you and your family are. As it turns out, Cardinal O'Connor read all about Jimmy's murder in the newspapers. Here's the good news. Cardinal O'Connor is coming to Saint Joseph's Church to attend the mass and give the eulogy for Jimmy on Saturday."

"Oh, that's wonderful news Owen," exclaimed Mary.

"Wait, there's more. The Cardinal also told me that Mayor David Dinkins and possibly Governor Mario Cuomo may also attend the service. Jimmy's murder has gotten a lot of public attention, and the politicians are lining up to get on the right side of this incident."

"Whether the reason for all these important men are coming is political or it's God's hand at work, it's still a miracle and my prayers have been answered," Mary said. "Nobody knew who my Jimmy was in life. I just wish he could know how much attention was being paid to him now."

Chapter 38 - Don't Know Nothing About No Murder

MICHAEL TAYLOR AND Philip Sarlo had kept a low profile since murdering Jimmy Zappalorti on Sunday night. As they walked up Androvette Street that night, they looked at the costume jewelry and gold chalice they stole from the Zappalorti home and decided most of it was not worth hocking. They only kept the cash and threw the other stuff away on the street. They stayed at a friend's house in the South Beach section of Staten Island. They were reading the newspapers and watching the TV news and knew that the police were on their trail. On January 24, 1990, they sat around aimlessly drinking beers at the Surfside Bar in South Beach. It was 6:30 P.M. and the January wind was blowing off the Atlantic Ocean on the northeast shore of Staten Island. The bar was poorly lit, smoky, and smelled like stale beer and potato chips. A football game played on the large color television.

A couple of drunks, three skin heads and their girlfriends sat at the bar drinking and watching the game. Hidden in the back of the bar in a dark booth, Taylor and Sarlo sipped their beers.

"What the fuck are we gonna do, Mike?" Sarlo asked.

"The old woman didn't see a damn thing," Taylor said. "It was too dark! How many times do I have go over this. The cops got nothing to tie us to the murder."

Sarlo was obsessed by Mary's potential ability to identify them and by getting to the bottom of why Taylor had to kill Jimmy. Taylor maintained a cavalier attitude, claiming the police should give them a medal for terminating "one more queer."

"We gotta get out of here," Sarlo worried. "I've got this place in Ocala, Florida, see…"

"Screw Florida," yelled Taylor! "There ain't any reason to run away, idiot!"

Suddenly, two uniformed policemen entered the smoke filled bar. They looked around, then walked over towards the bar. One of the pair handed a photograph to the bartender. Then they approached the "skinheads," who took a look at the pictures, threw them on the floor and continued watching the football game.

"Just sit tight. Don't panic," Taylor said. "Soon as they turn their backs, slip out of the booth and go into the john. Now, go, go!"

Sarlo and Taylor slowly slip out of the booth. They entered the bathroom, which was covered in graffiti and caked filth. Quietly, Taylor locked the door behind them. He turned and signaled Sarlo to be quiet by placing his index finger on his lips.

After distributing the photos of Taylor and Sarlo to all the patrons in the bar, the policemen walked outside and noted a dark sedan parked in the corner of the lot. Detectives Bergin and Jensen were in the front seat.

"What do you think, Sam?" asked Detective Bergin.

"Soon as we started passing out the pictures, two scumbags snuck into the crapper," Sam reported. "I think they're your guys."

"I knew this would flush 'em out. Good job," Jensen said, smiling. "Stay close as back-up. When they come out of the bar we'll to arrest 'em."

Sam nodded. He and the other police officer walked over to their squad car, got in, and pulled the car to the rear of the lot.

When Sarlo and Taylor exited the restroom, the bartender handed them their booking photos from their 1986 arrest.

"Oh, shit," Taylor exhaled.

"Man I told you," Sarlo complained.

"I didn't tell 'em jack shit," the bartender said.

Pointing to the other patrons in the bar, Taylor asked, "What about them?"

"They couldn't care less," the bartender said. "Did you really snuff that fag the other night?"

"Shut the fuck up and mind your business," Taylor advised. He grabbed Sarlo by his sleeve and dragged him to the front of the bar.

"Now, listen," Taylor said, "Here's our story: We don't know nothin' about no murder. We found the keys on the sidewalk in front of the Zappalorti house. We thought we would use them and steal something."

"Are you crazy?" Sarlo replied. "We'll get arrested for burglary!"

"Not when you use keys," Taylor proclaimed.

"We'll still draw time," Sarlo complained.

"Probably same as last time! Right?" Taylor said.

"You do what you want Mike, but I won't be part of it," Sarlo said. "I'm getting the fuck out of town, so they can't find me. I'm not going back to jail for you or anyone else. I'll die in jail. Give me half the cash. I'm going' to Florida."

"No, you ain't," Taylor threatened. "You're staying right here so I can keep an eye on you."

"Let's just get outta this bar, Mike," Sarlo said.

"Now that's the first smart thing you've said all day," Taylor replied.

Phil Sarlo and Mike Taylor headed for the front door of the bar. They started to walk across the parking lot. Immediately, the detectives drove at them from one side of the lot and the two uniformed police officers cut them off from the other side. Detectives Bergin and Jensen jumped out of the car. Likewise, the two uniformed policemen also got out of their car with their guns drawn.

Detective Bergin yelled, "Freeze! Get down on your stomachs! On the ground! Now!" Instead of following the police officer's commands, the murderers ran back into the bar. Detectives Bergin and Jensen pursued. The two remaining policemen jumped into their car, raced around to the back of the building, and shone their spotlight on the back door.

When the detectives entered the Surfside Bar, Taylor and Sarlo were desperately seeking a place to hide.

"Taylor! Sarlo! Stop now!" Bergin commanded! "I'll shoot! Stop!"

The bartender and his patrons all ran for cover. Taylor leapt on a chair and sprinted up onto the bar. He grabbed what liquor bottles he could reach and threw them at Detectives Bergin and Jensen. One of the bottles hit Jensen squarely in the face. Blood splattered as the bottle broke. Jensen fell to the floor unconscious. Bergin fired his handgun at Taylor but missed. A bottle of whiskey exploded all over the bartender, who lay on the floor. Detectives Bergin aimed his gun at Taylor, who threw another liquor bottle at him. He ducked it, as aimed his hand gun and fired, grazing Taylor's leather jacket. In that moment, Sarlo dashed back into the bathroom and locked the door.

In the bathroom, Sarlo looked around, glanced up at the ceiling, and saw a trapdoor. Then he opened the window, stood on the sink, and kicked out the screen. He came back down, turned, and jumped up on the toilet bowl. He pushed back a plywood panel that led to an attic loft, hauled himself up into the loft and slid the plywood back into place.

While Sarlo was hiding in the attic, Taylor was busy fighting for his life in the bar. Detective Jensen had regained consciousness and was reorient himself while wiping blood dripping from his forehead. Taylor, still standing on the bar had pulled out the same knife he used to kill Jimmy. Detective Bergin took a shot at him, but just missed the nervously-shifting target, hitting a bottle of Russian Vodka. Taylor leapt from the bar, aiming for Bergin. He landed directly on the detective. His momentum drove Bergin down. Taylor tried to jam the knife into Bergin's left shoulder, but the detective held his hand back. Bergin slammed him on the right side of the head with his pistol. Taylor grabbed the pistol and tried to wrest it free. When Detective Jensen saw Bergin in trouble, he grabbed a chair, came up behind Taylor and whacked him hard. He knocked Taylor off of his partner and then wrenched the knife out of Taylor's hand. He rolled Taylor over on his stomach while holding his hands together. Bergin managed to find his handcuffs and get them on Taylor. Bergin, screamed, "Where's Sarlo?

"He locked himself in the bathroom," Jensen informed. "Help me kick the door down."

Detectives Bergin and Jensen ran to the bathroom and kicked at the door until it burst open. They looked around, surprised not to find Sarlo. Both are duped by the open window and broken screen. They hurried to the bar, and Bergin pulled Mike Taylor off the floor.

"Where did Sarlo say he was going?" Detective Bergin demanded.

Taylor snarled a string of expletives.

Bergin ran outside and to tell Sam and Charlie to search for Sarlo. He found the pair of cops guarding the back door with their guns drawn.

"Did you see any sign of Philip Sarlo?"

"No, we were standing here the whole time, and no one came out," Sam said.

"He climbed out the bathroom window, so look around for him," Detective Bergin said.

The two police officers split up and began searching the general area. Detective Bergin went back inside to help his partner. As he entered the bar, Detective Jensen asked, "Where's Sarlo?" Detective Bergin shrugged. "Can't find him. He's gone!"

On the roof a metal trap door slid open. Phil Sarlo stuck his head out. He looked around and then slowly crawled out. He stood up and carefully slid the trap door back in place. Then he walked to the edge of the roof. From his high vantage point, he could see the two policemen searching around the building with flashlights. Sarlo quietly walked to the opposite side of the bar. He noticed a sturdy metal drainpipe mounted on the corner of the building. He shimmed down the pipe and looked around. He then took off running and disappeared into the darkness.

Chapter 39 - The Last Time I Saw Him Alive

AT 1:00 P.M. the following day, Robert went to visit his parents in Charleston. He parked his car and walked to the front of the stained glass studio. As he approached, he could see through the window that the lights were on over the work benches and someone was in there. He tested the door, found it unlocked, and opened it. Once inside he saw his father, Michael leaning over a wood bench meticulously soldering each lead joint of a stained glass window. Robert walked into the studio. Michael placed the hot iron onto a metal tray with a rack to hold the tool safely.

"It's beautiful," Robert admired.

Michael wheeled around, caught by surprise. His initial reaction of surprise softened. He turned back to the stained glass window on the bench.

"Oh, hi Bobby. I gotta work," he explained. "If I stop, I think too much about Jimmy. No work today?"

"No Pop, I took a few days off to be with you and mom, and learn more about why Jimmy was murdered," Robert said.

Well, I have good news. The police arrested Michael Taylor last night."

"That is good news," Robert said. "Now maybe the police can get more details."

Mike set down a piece of solder. "I read it in this morning's Staten Island Advance. I'm glad they caught the lousy bastard. Would you like a beer?"

"Sure Pop, I'll have one," Robert said.

Michael takes two beers from a small fridge along the wall of the studio. "Miller okay? The can of Budweiser on the bench was Jimmy's. I'm saving it."

"Dad, can you tell me what went on the afternoon of Jimmy's murder? What was Jimmy's mood that day," Robert asked?

Mike leaned against a wall. "Funny you should ask, because that's what I was thinking about when you walked in the studio. I've been thinking about that day, over and over again. It was the last time I saw Jimmy alive."

Mike began recounting the events of January 22, 1990. "I was fixing dinner in the kitchen for your mother, while she rested in her bedroom. At about 5:00 P.M. I heard Jimmy's key in the lock of the front door. According to the police, Jimmy had the confrontation with Taylor and Sarlo that afternoon in front of the grocery store around 4:00 P.M. I guess Jimmy had already put the incident out of his mind by the time he came home. I wish he'd told me about it. Jimmy just put the groceries away without saying a word.

Oh yeah, I remember he purchased cigarettes and a six pack of Bud." Michael took a sip of his beer, then continued, "All he said to us was, 'While going to the store, I spoke to Carol Kosa. Then I stopped for a cigarette when I was leaving the grocery store.' I can't understand why he never told us about Taylor and Sarlo harassing him."

"What time did you last see Jimmy that day?" Robert asked.

"It was about 6:45 P.M. You know, Bobby, I saw the picture of Michael Taylor in today's newspaper. It's right on the front page. After seeing his picture, I remember him and another man standing in front of the Wagon Wheel bar that night. The second one was probably Phillip Sarlo. Had I known, I could have confronted them. Stopped them from killing Jimmy a few hours later."

Michael looked up at the lone can of Budweiser beer on his work bench. His stern face softened, and tears started to flow down his cheeks. He cried passionately.

Robert leaned over and placed his arm around his father. "Dad, neither you nor anyone else in our family had any idea that these two men were bullying Jimmy. Don't beat yourself up over it. Maybe Jimmy thought he could defend himself from these guys. You shouldn't feel guilty about not knowing what was going on, or for not being able to help Jimmy. We all could have stopped his murder, if we had only known beforehand. We don't have crystal balls to look into the future."

Michael wiped the tears from his eyes, "Yeah, that's good advice. How could Mickey or I have known? Thanks, Bobby." Michael shook his son's hand and attempted a smile.

The side door of the studio opened and Peggy ran into the workshop. "Dad! They want Mom down at the 122nd Precinct right away. The police got one of them and they want Mom to confirm and identify him!"

208

Chapter 40 - Because Jimmy Wasn't Afraid

AFTER RECEIVING MEDICAL treatment at Staten Island Hospital for the wounds they received while arresting Mike Taylor the night before, Detectives Jensen and Bergin prepared to question their prisoner. They had Taylor brought from the holding cell to the interrogation room at the 122nd Precinct. The time was 4:00 P.M. The interrogation room was painted a dull gray and had the usual mirror on one wall where outside observers might look in unseen. Michael Taylor's hands were cuffed in front of him; he was seated at a table. Jensen had bandages over the cuts on his forehead and nose, and Bergin was angry at Taylor for what he had done to his partner. They began questioning their prisoner.

"Look at Detective Jensen's face," Detective Bergin railed. "Four stitches! That alone is gonna get you five years in the can!"

"That ain't gonna get me shit," Taylor riposted. "It was self defense, so fuck off!"

"You killed Jimmy Zappalorti," Jensen accused, "and we can prove it!"

Taylor stared at him defiantly. "I didn't kill nobody."

"Then what the hell were you doing with his keys?"

"I never saw that shit before," Taylor said.

"Your prints are all over them."

"We found them on the street," Taylor said. "In front of his house, that's all."

"That ain't all," Detective Bergin said! "You and Sarlo broke into the Zappalorti house to rip them off!"

"You can't break into a house if you got keys," Taylor argued.

The session went on in the same direction, with Bergin and Jensen presenting the knife and Jimmy's blood as damning evidence while Taylor was demanding a lawyer. Suddenly a red light flashed above the mirror. Detective Bergin exited the interrogation room.

Detective Bergin entered the adjoining observation room. The curtain was closed, so no one could see what was going on inside the interrogation room.

A uniformed police officer had escorted Mary, Michael, Mickey, Peggy and Robert into the observation room. Detective Bergin pulled the curtain open so all can see into the connecting room.

"What do you think, Mary? Is that the man who was in your house?"

"Yes, Detective, he's one of the two men that were in my house," Mary replied. "He's the one who used the telephone. He's the one with the evil eyes!"

Detective Bergin said confidently, "He'll confess. You just wait."

He turned and walked back toward the interrogation room. Taylor eyed Detective Bergin as he went to a file cabinet and pulled out some criminal file jackets. He threw them on the table in front of Taylor.

"Know what this is? Back in 1986, you beat a homosexual man almost to death with a crowbar. You and your pal, Sarlo were convicted."

Taylor replied, "I only did a year!"

"But two time losers start at twenty years," Detective Jensen told him. "And for first-degree murder it's probably life. With your young body, I wouldn't want to be up in Sing-Sing forever."

"I want a lawyer?" Taylor said.

"You got an ax to grind concerning homosexuality? Is that what happened when you were locked up in 1986?" Jensen asked. "Some huge stud make you his bitch? Didn't you like it, pretty boy?"

Detective Jensen continued, "Some stud turn you into a girly-boy?"

"Get me a lawyer!"

"We got your fingerprints on a pile of stuff in Jimmy's shack."

"So what," Taylor said? "What does that prove?"

"It places you at the scene of the crime," Detective Bergin said. "Plus, you got a history of hating and bashing gays."

"You got a prison record for assaulting a gay man," Detective Jensen added.

"You're going up for murder!" Bergen said.

"Not only that, but you're swallowing the whole fish by yourself. You're dead meat, unless you cop a plea."

"This whole thing was Sarlo's idea, not mine!" Taylor blurted out. "I just wanted to kick his ass. Sarlo wanted to kill him, he did the whole thing. I just wanted to beat him up and take his money. That's all, I swear!"

The moment had now come to capture the confession on video and audio tapes. Taylor was a poster boy for the 'No honor among thieves' criminal type. Detective Bergin turned on the recording devices. He pointed at Taylor and said, "Start talking."

Michael Taylor looked at the two detectives, paused for a moment and then said, "It went down this way, uh, um. We'd been watching him you know, the queer guy, Jimmy. He was always strutting his stuff around the neighborhood. We didn't want a bunch a fags moving into Charleston. You know what I mean? So, we decided to teach him a lesson, so that night we went to his shack. You know, to that shack he built by the river."

Without coaxing, Taylor recalled the details of the attack, finding Jimmy reading in the bedroom, the back and forth fight, the baseball bat, the wallet that Jimmy flung into the bushes. And then the knife.

"Phil stabbed the knife into his chest. I yelled for him not to do it. We don't want to kill him!"

Jensen snapped. "That's a lie! Sarlo's fingerprints aren't on the knife. Only yours are on it, you get no deal unless you tell us the truth!"

Mike Taylor knew that he was caught lying. He paused for a moment, then resumed his account.

"Well yeah, it was me who plunged the knife into the fag's chest. So when I stabbed him, he yelled, 'Stop! Stop!' But I stabbed him a few more times. I wanted to make sure he would die. I grabbed his hair, pulled his head back and I slit his throat. Then I dropped the queer and left him there on the ground, bleeding. We had to hide his body, so we thought the best way was to throw him in the river and he'd wash out to sea."

Taylor went on in cold detachment, describing their clumsy attempt to get the body into the water, then to find money and a flashlight. Failing this, to use Jimmy's keys to rob his house. Taylor shrugged as if apologizing for stealing a piece of candy and said, "And that's how it all went down."

"Why did you have to kill him?! Tell me," Detective Jensen asked!

"Come on, speak up Taylor," Detective Bergin encouraged.

Taylor put his cuffed hands to his face and rubbed his closed eyes and cheeks. He paused in thought, then the murderer looked at the detectives and knew that he had to come clean.

"Because he wasn't afraid! Fags are supposed to be gutless. I wanted him to cry. I wanted him to act like a crying homo, but he wouldn't. He just kept fighting back! Why the hell didn't he act like a fag?" With Taylor's twisted logic revealed, Detectives Jensen and Bergin relaxed their interrogation. The tape recorder and video camera were still running and captured what Taylor admitted. "I wouldn't have killed him if he just had begged me," Taylor emphasized.

Detective Bergin dialed the phone. A minute later, two uniformed police officers entered the interrogation room and grabbed Michael Taylor. "Let me know when the Public Defender gets here," Bergen instructed. The two policemen and Taylor exited the room. Taylor said nothing, offered no words of remorse. Then he was led away.

Detectives Bergin and Jensen came out of the interrogation room and joined the Zappalorti family. "His goose is cooked," Detective Jensen said. "We'll get Phil Sarlo too."

Michael Zappalorti came up to Detectives Jensen and Bergin and shook their hands. Then Mickey and Robert also came over and thanked the two detectives for a job well done.

"Mike, you, Mickey, and Peggy get the car," Mary instructed. "Bobby and I are going to have a word with the detectives."

The trio left. Mary and Robert sat down on chairs and motioned for the detectives to come to her. They stood in front of her.

"Detectives Bergin and Jensen, I want to thank you for the extra effort you put into finding Jimmy's murderer," Mary said. "You've both suffered from the hands of Michael Taylor when you arrested him."

Surprised and touched by her perception, "We were just doing our jobs, Mrs. Zappalorti, Detective Bergin said." While Detective Jensen nodded in agreement.

"No, you guys went above and beyond your normal investigative tasks to help my family, and I know it. So, thank you from the bottom of my heart," Mary said. "I'll keep you both in my prayers."

"If you guys were not on the ball for the first forty-eight hours, you may not have caught Taylor," Robert said. "So I too thank you for taking an extra interest in my brother's murder."

Detectives Bergin and Jensen were humbled and expressed their thanks to the Zappalorti family members. Mary took her son Robert's arm as they both walked to the exit of the 122nd police station. Michael, Mickey and Peggy were waiting at the curb in the parked car. The family drove off and returned to their Charleston home.

Chapter 41 - In Jimmy's Name

ROBERT WANTED TO attend a memorial service that Jimmy's friends were having at the Pink Flamingo. It would give him a chance to speak with Don Shepler to learn more about Jimmy's other gay life. His oldest son Bobby, Jr.'s band Lonely Nights in Paris was also performing at the memorial. He made arrangements to meet Don at the Pink Flamingo bar in Manhattan the following evening. The Pink Flamingo bar was near the corner of Christopher Street and 7th Avenue South in the Village. Robert was rested, clean shaven and his hair was neatly combed. He was dressed in a blue shirt, black slacks and black shoes. He had a black leather jacket over the blue shirt. The vehicular traffic on the New York City street created its own cacophonous melody, mixing with blaring jukebox dance music. Gay couples of both sexes walked past Robert. Some of them went into the Pink Flamingo Bar. He stood in front of the bar for a moment thinking how many times Jimmy was probably here.

Robert noticed an announcement on the marquee and a big sign in the window that read: Special Memorial Tonight for Our Late Friend – James P. Zappalorti. Robert looked around for a moment, then entered the bar. The club was filled with people, but the atmosphere was subdued and the dance floor empty. Most of the stools at the bar were filled with chatting patrons. All the tables were also filled. On the stage platform sat the baby grand piano, draped in black and purple cloth. The cloth was covered by dozens of cards, pictures, flowers and newspaper clippings about Jimmy's murder. In the middle of the shrine was a picture of Jimmy playing the same piano.

He saw his son, Bobby, Jr., and three other band members, Rich, Gill and Harry setting-up their instruments and microphones next to the piano. Robert walked to the bar and put down a five dollar bill. Bernie Bristol, the bartender, filled his order for a coke with lemon. Bobby walked over to his father and greeted him. They spoke for a moment then Bobby said, "Listen Dad, we're about to start the ceremony for Jimmy. I'd like you to say a few words about Jimmy before we start to play if you don't mind?

Surprised by his son's request, Robert nonetheless said. "Sure, I'll be happy to."

"Great, Dad." Bobby went back to the stage and grabbed the microphone. "May I have your attention please? I'd like to thank everyone for coming out tonight to honor the memory of my late uncle, James Patrick Zappalorti. You knew him as Jimmy. This is my first time at the Pink Flamingo, but I felt it would be appropriate to honor his memory here, and introduce an original song I wrote for him." Bobby paused for a moment, picked up a glass and took a drink of water, then looked out at the assembled people in the club.

"Before I sing my song, I'd like to introduce my father, and Jimmy's older brother, Robert Zappalorti. Dad would you say a few words to the audience," Bobby said pointing to his Dad.

Robert walked to the stage and took the microphone in his hand. "Good evening everyone. There are so many people I want to thank for all the help they have given the Zappalorti family. Among them are Matt Foreman, from the New York City Gay and Lesbian Anti-Violence Project. Matt's group offered a $5,000.00 reward for the capture of Philip Sarlo, one of my brother's murderers. Matt, is involved in trying to get the 'Hate Crimes Bill' passed in Albany." Robert adjusted the microphone and looked out at the audience and continued.

"For the past year, the gay community has been trying to assist legislators and politicians to get a hate crimes bill passed in the New York State Senate. The 'Hate Crimes Bill' has been blocked by some Republican politicians based upon only two words in the legislation. Those words are: 'sexual orientation.' While Matt and the gay community struggle to get the bill passed, thousands of New Yorkers, including over 6,000 lesbian and gay people in New York City alone, have become victims of hate violence. Those hate crime victims in general, and my brother Jimmy Zappalorti in particular, demand in spirit that we get this bill signed into law. So, with your help and support, let's get the 'Hate Crimes Bill' passed!"

The crowed sprang from their seats, cheered, waved their arms, and applauded for many seconds. Robert took a sip of his Coke and put the microphone up to his mouth again, he said, "I'd also like to thank Dr. Patrick J. Suraci, a professional counselor who is helping my family cope with the murder of Jimmy. Finally, I'd be remiss if I didn't thank Bert Coffman, who is starting a nonprofit, active support group for lesbian, gay, bisexual, or transgendered people who suffered from mental illness. Bert has my mother's blessing to organize his group named 'The Zappalorti Society' in Jimmy's honor."

The audience clapped and cheered, giving a strong supportive applause. "Before I turn the stage over to my son's band, I just want to thank Don Shepler and Lou Epstein, Jimmy's closest Manhattan friends."

Robert pointed to Don, but he broke down sobbing. He put his head onto Lou's shoulder. Lou hugged and comforted his friend. The audience gave a respectful round of applause and then lapsed into silence.

"Thank you everyone for remembering my brother, Jimmy. Now, here's my son's band, Lonely Nights in Paris," Robert concluded.

The band members readied their instruments and checked the levels on the sound system. Bobby stepped up to the microphone

218

and said, "I wrote this song sitting in Jimmy's beach house. I was inspired by his spiritual presence and the fond memories I have for my uncle. The song is titled: 'In Jimmy's Name.'"

With his guitar in hand, Gill on drums, Rich on bass, and Harry on keyboard, Bobby began.

Jimmy loved to roam...but he never found his way.
Always on his own...he knew no other way.
People's hatred is something that Jimmy could not understand.
He built his own Beach House, enjoyed the simple life.
Until that dreadful day, when someone took his life.
People's hatred is something that, Jimmy could not understand.
Heaven called, and an angel came, and took him away.
Won't you put your hands together. In Jimmy's name.
Put your hands together, in Jimmy's name.
Heaven called, and an angel came...Jimmy...Jimmy!
More than a friend, he was someone that I loved.
Now that he's gone, his memory lives on.
His memory lives on, and on, and on, and on...
He lay there in the sand, blood washed upon the shore.
I reached out for his hand, but I couldn't help no more.
Why don't we get together and just accept each other for who we are.
I sat in his Beach House, and watched the sun go down.
I can still see him standing there...but Jimmy's not around.
Why don't we get together and just accept each other for who we are.
Heaven called, and an angel came, and took him away.
Won't you put your hands together, In Jimmy's name

As Bobby sang the words, everyone in the audience stood. They all held their hands above their heads while swaying to the rhythm of the music and sang along with Bobby.

Put your hands together...In Jimmy's name.

Won't you put your hands together...in Jimmy's name.
"Put your hands together...In Jimmy's name.
Won't you put your hands together...in Jimmy's name.

Bobby strummed the last few notes while everyone applauded. All were noticeably moved by the emotional song. A few cried. The band then played another original song dedicated to Jimmy called, "Kiss and Tell."

After the second song was finished, Bobby told the audience members, "Thank you folks. Thanks to everyone for coming out tonight. Good night!"

While patrons congratulated the band members on their nice performance and special songs, Robert went to the bar and ordered another drink. Then he walked over to Don and Lou's table to join them. Don stood up and greeted Robert. They hugged for a moment and sat down.

"Nice to see you guys again," Robert said.

"Good to see you too, Bob. I just wish it were under better circumstances," Don said.

"Your son's song is amazing. It made us cry," Lou said.

"Yeah, he's a talented musician and composer. He's better than I ever was at playing guitar," Robert said. Changing the subject he asked Don, "How well did you know Jimmy?

"I loved him," Don said, his voice trailing away.

"But did you really know him," Robert asked?

"I think, nobody really knew him, but everybody loved him. You know, Jimmy would come in here with that angel's smile and make this piano sing. He was an amazing guy. Wasn't scared of anything. I don't think he knew how to be scared. Just trusted that everybody was good. He was like a child. Oh, jeez, I'm gonna miss him!"

Lou nodded in agreement and Don began to tear up. He cupped his face with his hands. Robert looked at Don and placed his hand on his shoulder.

"How did you meet Jimmy," Robert asked?

They talked about the first encounter and several other things, eventually landing on the subject of all the muggings Jimmy suffered traveling from Staten Island to Manhattan.

"Jimmy just shrugged them off," Don said, "as if…"

"As if what?" Robert pushed.

"As if he thought he deserved it," Don answered. "Maybe because nobody in power cared enough to make sure everybody understands that hating is wrong. We gay people have rights too!"

"I couldn't agree with you more, Don," Robert said. "I have a selfish reason for wanting gay people to have rights and be treated with respect."

"Why is that, Bob," Don asked curiously?

"Because my youngest son, Michael also happens to be gay," Robert informed. "I don't want my son being beaten or killed the same way my brother was."

"That's right, Jimmy told me that your son was gay," Don said. "I had forgotten."

Listen, are you and Lou going to attend Jimmy's funeral this Saturday on Staten Island?"

"Of course we are, Bob. We wouldn't miss it," Don exclaimed.

"Good, I'll see you guys there. Let me buy you guys another glass of wine before I go."

"You don't have to do that, Bob," Lou said.

"My treat for my brother's best friends," Robert said. "Goodbye, Don. Bye, Lou."

The men shook hands and Robert walked to the bar and put a twenty dollar bill down in front of the bartender.

"Another round of drinks for Don and Lou, please," Robert said.

"You need change?" Bernie asked.

"More than you'll ever know," Robert replied as he pushed the money back to the bartender. "Listen, you knew Jimmy, right?"

Bernie swiped the bar with his cloth and said, "Sure I knew him.

I remember the first time he ever came in the bar years ago. Why do you ask?"

"I know that he played piano here," Robert replied. "But, I'm wondering if he hung around any other clubs. Jimmy once told me he also went to the Ramrod."

"Yeah, Jimmy told me he went to the Ramrod Club, too," Bernie said.

"Where's that," Robert asked?

"It's at 349 West Street." Bernie said. "But if you believe in hell, you won't go there."

"I just wanted to see it for myself. Maybe someone will remember Jimmy," Robert said.

"Jimmy had more guts than brains. Leave it at that," Bernie said. "My advice is don't go to the Ramrod. They probably won't even let a straight dude like you in the door, so why waste your time!"

"Jimmy also told me he went to a piano bar called The Monster," Robert said. "Where's that?"

"Yeah, that's a nice place on Sheridan Square. It's at 80 Grove Street, and not too far from here in the West Village," Bernie informed.

Robert placed two more dollars on the bar.

Bernie said, "Thanks, Bob."

Robert exited the Pink Flamingo and walked to the corner. He hailed an approaching taxicab. The cab stopped. He opened the door. "Do you know where The Monster is?"

"Yeah, three blocks west and two blocks south. Get in," the cabbie said.

"Thanks," Robert slammed the cab door shut.

"Asshole!" the cabbie yelled as he sped away.

"No question about it," Robert said to himself. He started walking to the West Side of Manhattan.

Chapter 42 - Never Mind Where I Am

PHILIP SARLO HAD taken a Greyhound Bus from the Port Authority Bus Terminal in Manhattan all the way to Ocala, in Marion County, Florida. He had a friend down there who he had met in jail in 1986, a guy he thought he could stay with and hide out for a while. Sarlo did not find his friend at the address he had, and the phone number was disconnected, so he was forced to stay at a motel, seriously draining his money. Sarlo had called his brother Stephen, who lived on Staten Island. Stephen assured him the cops were hot on his trail. His brother also told him that two detectives had came to his house looking for Phil. Sarlo's brother advised Phil to call Detective Jensen and gave him the phone number on Jensen's business card, but Sarlo said, "I'm not ready to speak with the cops yet," and hung up.

On February 18, 1990, out of desperation, Sarlo called a friend back on Staten Island to ask him to borrow some money. Since the friend was after the $15,000.00 reward money, he told Sarlo he'd try to get some money together for him, but he had to call him back in four hours. On that day, Detectives Bergin and Jensen were working the four-to-twelve shift in the Crimes against Persons Squad at the 122nd Precinct. For several days they had been tracking down leads on Sarlo from informants who looked to collect the reward money. Detective Jensen's phone rang. Sergeant Dennis Casavillo was on the line.

"Bob, an unnamed informant and acquaintance of Sarlo told me that he had received a telephone call at home today from Sarlo."

"No shit! That's great."

Casavillo continued, "Yeah, and he said that Sarlo was going to call him again at 6:00 P.M. this evening."

"Give me his name and address, and we'll go there before the suspect calls him back again," Detective Jensen said.

Jensen called the informant's house and made arrangements to go there with his partner, Detective Bergin. Within half an hour they were at the informant's house waiting for Sarlo's phone call. Twenty minutes later, the phone rang and the informant answered. The caller was Philip Sarlo. The informant told Sarlo that someone wanted to speak to him and handed, Detective Jensen the phone. He had to choose his words carefully, so Sarlo would not hang up. After identifying himself, Detective Jensen said, "Phil, I have a deal I want to make with you, so hear me out."

With no other options, no friends and no money, Philip Sarlo decided to speak. Jensen let him do most of the talking. Sarlo spoke at length before Jensen was able to broach the subject of his whereabouts.

"Listen Phil, why don't you come over to the 122nd precinct and make a declaration," Detective Jensen suggested. "Or we can send a squad car and pick you up. Where are you?"

"Never mind where I am," Sarlo said. "I'm telling you the whole thing was Taylor's idea! I never wanted to kill the guy!"

"Okay, I believe you, Phil, but you have to tell me where you are, so we can work out the details face to face," Detective Jensen said.

At first, Sarlo claimed he was in Georgia. Next, he told Jensen he was in Tampa, Florida. With more prompting, he finally admitted he was in a phone booth in Ocala, Florida.

"It's at a Burger King restaurant parking lot. I'm about a block from the junction of Interstate 75 and State Route 40. If we can work something out I'll turn myself in. I want to come back to New

York. I'm tired of running."

Jensen beckoned Detective Bergin to approach. He wrote in big letters on a note pad: Go next store and ask to use the phone. Call the Ocala police department in Florida and tell them to pick-up Philip Sarlo on a homicide warrant. He's in a phone booth at a Burger King near the junction of Route 40 and Interstate 75.

Bergin gave his partner the thumbs-up sign, then wrote a message back to Detective Jensen: Keep him on the line while I call from next door. Bergin hurried to a neighbor's door, identified himself, and used their telephone. In short order, he had been connected with the Ocala Police Department.

Meantime, Detective Jensen keep Sarlo on the phone by discussing a plea bargain. He chose his words cautiously as he spoke.

"So Phil, what do you want to do," Detective Jensen asked? "Are you ready to turn yourself in?"

"No, not yet! I just want to convince you that Taylor did the stabbing, not me. I'll swear to it. Will that help me with a deal?"

"First, tell me in detail what happened. Leave out nothing. Right from that afternoon," Jensen prompted.

While Sarlo was pleading his case, a marked Ocala Police vehicle driven by Officer Kenneth Sumner and accompanied by Detective Stephen Thibodeau, drove quietly into the Burger King parking lot. They two police officers spotted Sarlo in the phone booth. The car moved slowly toward the phone booth.

"No! No deal," Sarlo argued. "I won't go for that!" As he spoke, Sarlo looked to his left and saw the Ocala Police car closing in.

"Oh shit!" Sarlo yelled. He dropped the handset, dashed out of the phone booth, and ran away from the police car. Sarlo ran as fast as he could down Route 40. The police car gave chase, cut him off, and forced Sarlo between a parked car and a store front. Sarlo slammed into the hood of the police car. As the cops opened their doors, he ran back toward the Burger King. Sumner and Thibodeau jumped out of the car and gave chase. Sarlo dashed inside the Burger

King and o grabbed a young woman from a table. He whipped out a knife and held it to her throat. The officers ran into the Burger King with their pistols drawn.

"Get out of here," Phil Sarlo demanded! "Leave me alone or I'm going to cut her throat! Go on! I'll kill her! I swear it! I'll kill her!"

Behind Sarlo stood a formidable black man named Leroy Garner. Garner was a former defensive lineman on the University of Florida football team. He was dressed in a Burger King manager's uniform.

Leroy held a small wooden baseball bat in his right hand. Leroy swung the bat into Sarlo's head. The force of the blow sent the criminal to the floor.

"You ain't gonna cut nobody in my Burger King," Leroy declared, looking down at the unconscious, bleeding murderer.

An hour later, in the Homicide Room at the 122nd Precinct in Staten Island, New York, Detective Bergin spoke on the telephone to Detective Stephen Thibodeau of the Ocala Police Department. Detective Jensen stood next to him.

Bergin said, "That's great! We'll start extradition right away. The New York City Police Department owes the Ocala Police Department a favor, big time. Thanks Detective Thibodeau." Bergin hung up the phone and turned to Jensen. "The Ocala police have Phil Sarlo in a holding cell," Detective Bergin said. "Detective Thibodeau promised to personally escort Sarlo back to New York. Call the Zappalorti family and let them know."

In 2004, Robert Zappalorti, Sr. moved to Florida. He purchased a three-bedroom home on five acres of land in Dunnellon, just fifteen miles west of Ocala. He had the opportunity to speak with Detective Stephen Thibodeau of the Ocala Police Department, who gave him copies of the Marion County arrest documents and other details of Sarlo's arrest and extradition back to Staten Island, New York, and provided specifics for this chapter.

Chapter 43 - I Never Said Goodbye to Him

ROBERT WAS AT his parents' home on February 19, 1990, when the call came through that Philip Sarlo had been captured. He and his mother talked about the good news for some time, and then she said, "Bobby, I want you to help me do something."

"What mom, you should get some rest," he told her.

"No, that's all I do is rest," Mary said. "You're gonna take me down to Jimmy's beach house."

"Now," Robert said. "It's dark and cold down there."

"He's right, Mary," Michael interjected. "You can just about walk around the house, never mind walk all the way to the river."

"I want to say good-bye to Jimmy at the last place he was on earth. I never said good-bye to him. Mike, I want Bobby to walk me down there. You stay home and call Mickey and Peggy to let them know Sarlo was captured. Get my coat."

Mary's expression was resolute. As Michael went to the coat closet and got her coat, Robert put his coat on and then grabbed a flashlight from the counter. Mary took his arm, looked up at him and nodded. They exited the house from the front door as Michael went to the telephone and dialed Peggy's number. A minute later, Mary and Robert were on the sand road to Jimmy's shack. It was dark and cold as the January night air dropped to thirty-eight degrees, Fahrenheit. The road ahead was only illuminated by the beam of the flashlight and soft, bluish moon light. Although he moved slowly,

Mary struggled to keep up with her son, gasping for breath. They slowly approached Jimmy's shack.

Across the Arthur Kill River, the sound of a tugboat horn echoed in the night. The wind off the river kicked up and was blowing hard. Mary stopped, looked up at her middle son, and smiled weakly.

"Bobby, open the door for me. Then light the oil lanterns and some candles."

"Okay, Mom," Robert said. "Hold onto this tree while I go inside."

Robert pulled the door open and went into the shack. A moment later an uneven orange glow from the oil lamps and candles shined through the front door frame onto the ground at Mary's feet. Robert emerged and walked over to his mother.

"Now help me inside, but I want to be alone in there," Mary directed. "You can go back to the house and keep your father company. Come back in a half-hour; I'll be okay." They slowly walked to the door, and Mary went into Jimmy's shack.

Before closing the door, Robert glanced at Mary. She surveyed the room, taking in all Jimmy's possessions lying in piles on the table and on the floor as well as the posters of Italy, New York and San Francisco nailed to the walls. She walked up to the poster of Rome and reached out to touch it. She smiled.

"My Jimmy," Mary said aloud. "How you loved Rome. You enjoyed traveling so much. Always reading National Geographic magazines. You would show me the pictures of faraway places and tell me how you longed to go there."

Mary picked up various pictures. Some she clasped to her chest. For a time she stood in front of the picture window, imagining Jimmy's enjoyment at the restful scene.

Mary noticed a folded American flag on a milk crate, tucked away in the corner. She reached down and pulled the crate into the light of the lantern. She lifted the flag. Underneath, there lay a series of small stained glass windows in wood frames. There were also letters and postcards stuffed between the frames. She held one of the small windows up in the lantern light and admired its beauty. One was a replica of Jimmy's Navy photo. Another was a pink flamingo. Another was Jimmy in Rome in front of the Sistine Chapel. As she looked at small windows, she realized that each one represented an important moment in Jimmy's life.

Mary said aloud, "Why these are Jimmy's windows of life." She heard a knock on the door. The door slowly opened, and Robert poked his head inside.

"Dad told me to come back early. We were worried about you."

"I'm glad you did," Mary said. "Look at these windows Jimmy made."

Robert closed the door behind him and walked to his mother. "Wow, this is nice," Robert admired. "I never knew Jimmy could do such fine work with stained glass.

As far as I knew, Jimmy was the putty guy. He didn't show any talent for cutting glass or making glass designs. He must have made these windows at night when Mickey and Daddy were sleeping." Mary picked up another miniature stained glass picture of Jimmy playing piano, then handed it to Robert. Robert held it up to the light.

"What we never knew about Jimmy's talents," Robert marveled.

Mary held a window up for Robert to see. He shook his head slowly. Mary looked in the box and found some letters and post cards from Italy. She opened one of the letters and read it.

Robert picked up another small window and admired it. Then he picked up a cigar box and took out a handful of small smoothly polished round pieces of colored glass normally used as the center of flowers in stained glass windows or Tiffany lamps. Robert let the pieces run through his fingers as they dropped back into the box. Mary closed the letter and held it in her hand.

"Bobby, I want you to do a favor for me?"

"Sure anything, mom," Robert offered.

"I want you to read these letters and look at the photos," Mary requested. "You take them home with you. You never saw this letter that Jimmy wrote to me and your father while he was in Rome. It may encourage you to write a book about Jimmy someday. You know, tell his story."

Robert nodded and hugged his mother. Then he escorted her to the door. Mary took one last, lingering look, knowing she would probably never come to the shack again. Robert blew out the oil lamp and all the candles. The darkness and cold of death swept in.

Chapter 44 - The Pope's House in Rome

ROBERT ARRIVED AT his New Jersey home about one hour after he left his parent's house. He flicked on the light and placed the envelope on the end table next to his bed. He took off his shoes, shirt, and pants went into the bathroom and took shower. As he toweled off, he looked at himself in the mirror for moment, then walked back into his bedroom. Robert looked around his room until his gaze fixed on the large envelope with Jimmy's letters that his mother asked him to read. There were various papers, a series of photos of Jimmy with some friends, and a two-page letter. He looked through the photos. Robert admired the pictures of the Sistine Chapel, the fountain in Vatican City, and the gothic Rome churches. Robert picked up some other photographs capturing Jimmy with two handsome Italian men. The trio stood in Saint Peter's Square at the Vatican. Jimmy held some leaves from an olive tree. He next examined a round-trip ticket from La Guardia Airport in New York City to Leonardo da Vinci International Airport, in Rome.

Robert put the old ticket down and studied a couple of leaves that are carefully encased in a plastic zip-lock bag. He looked at them. Written on the bag in Jimmy's hand writing was a short note: Olive leaves from the Vatican Garden. They looked like the leaves Jimmy was holding in the photo. Finally, he came to the letter, written by Jimmy in his poor Spenserian handwriting. He began to read it aloud.

"Dear Mom and Dad: One of my dreams has come true for me. I'm here in Rome standing right in front of the Pope's House. Seeing it in person is far better than all the pictures I've seen in the National Geographic magazine. Dad, I'm so glad you loaned me your 35 mm camera. My two friends, Gianluca and Luigi are helping me take pictures.

Robert smiled. "'The Pope's House;' only you would say it that way, Jimmy."

There are thousands of people here in St. Peter's Square. I'm like a child in a candy store. I don't know what to go see first. My friends, Gianluca and Luigi are my tour guides. They are helping me see Vatican City. Dad, I want to thank you for all you taught me about stained glass windows. Knowing how much work that goes into making them, gives me a special appreciation of the beautiful stained glass windows here in the Sistine Chapel and in other cathedrals.

Mom, this place is almost like heaven. I feel happy, exhilarated and reborn. This feeling came over me when I looked up at the ceiling of the Sistine Chapel. Michelangelo's paintings are so real... it's like I'm looking at God. God's hand reached out to me. I feel God loves me now as both of you do. Daddy, I never thought I could make stained glass windows the way you and Mickey make them. Now I know I can. I have been inspired by God here at the Pope's House. I never want to leave this place. Every second I'm here, I feel I'm getting closer to God. Mom and Dad, do you think God would be angry at me if I make stained glass windows of my own life? Dad, I know I'm not as good as you and Mickey at making windows. Your work with glass is superior compared to mine. Dad, God gave you so much talent. You couldn't have made stained glass windows so good unless God was in you. Sometimes, I thought God hated me because I disrespected you. I didn't show up for work on time and I hit you Daddy. All those times when I argued with you, and made you angry. I also made Mother cry. There are Commandments against that you know?

Mom and Dad, please forgive me because sometimes I was a bad son. I'm really sorry.

"You're forgiven, Jimmy," Robert murmured. "You're forgiven." Then resumed reading the letter.

I now realize how lucky I am to have such loving parents like you. I have met and spoken to so many other gay men who were cast aside and rejected by their parents. But not me. You both stood by me because you love me. Because you loved me so much... I can accept who I am. I happen to be a gay man, but I'm gay because God made me this way. I didn't choose my life style... God chose it for me. Know what? God does not make mistakes. I except who I am and thank you both for accepting me. I'll see you when I get home.

Love always, Your Son, Jimmy

Robert smiled with satisfaction. He leaned back on his bed and closed his eyes. He thought about Jimmy and how happy he was in Rome. He started praying, "Our Father, who art in heaven…He heard a sound and opened his eyes, Jimmy appeared in his room.

"You praying for me, Bobby?"

"Yes, Jimmy. Do you want to pray with me?"

Jimmy nodded, bowed his head, and knelt. Robert prayed aloud.

"In the name of Father and of the Son and of the Holy Spirit, heal this child of Yours and let his soul become as flawless as the stained glass windows he has created. Amen."

"I never heard that prayer before," Jimmy said.

"I just made it up."

"Can you do that?"

"Sure I can. I'm a good Catholic."

"So am I. But I have to admit, I was a sinner."

Robert said, "Yes, Jimmy, I'm a sinner as well."

Jimmy reached out and took Robert's hands. "I want to tell you my secret. My secret is that when I die I don't want to go to heaven; I want to stay in one of Daddy's stained glass windows. You all made the stained glass windows with so much love. If I could just stay wrapped in their love forever, I'd be happy as one of the saints in the windows."

"You will Jimmy," Robert assured him. "You will, my brother."

Robert took Jimmy's right hand and shook it. Jimmy smiled at him and then began to slowly vanish. Suddenly, Robert was jolted awake by the sound of his alarm clock ringing. When he opened his eyes he realized he was sleeping on his bed. He knew that he was just dreaming, yet in his soul... that he had a visitation from his late brother. He looked around his bedroom. Jimmy's letter and photos were next to him on the bed. He had been dreaming amidst all Jimmy's memorabilia. He looked at his alarm clock. It was seven A.M., the day of Jimmy's memorial service in Saint Joseph's Church.

The service began at 10:00 A.M. in Rossville, Staten Island, and he did not want to be late. He stood awkwardly and went into the bathroom clean up. After shaving, showering and neatly combing his hair, Robert put on his neatly pressed shirt and black suit. He took the extra time to shine his shoes, wanting to look appropriate for the occasion. He felt good about himself and looked forward to spending the day with his beloved family.

Robert made the long drive from Ocean County, New Jersey, to Rossville, Staten Island. Saint Joseph's Church on Poplar Avenue was back-lit by a rising sun.

Chapter 45 - My Jimmy's in Heaven Now

IT WAS 9:45 in the morning. As far as the eye could see, Poplar Avenue was lined with vehicles: cars, news media vans, and a bus. Family and friends from all over New York City walked into the 142-year-old stone church. A black limo pulled up. The driver jumped out and opened the door for Cardinal John O'Connor and Monsignor Coheran. Newspaper photographers ran up and captured the moment. Another black limo pulled up behind the first one. Mayor David Dinkins got out, followed by his aids, Simon, Maryann, and Albert. Matt Forman greeted Mayor Dinkins and they spoke briefly. The Mayor and Cardinal O'Connor said hello to more media attention. They walked into the church together, followed by their entourage. The ordinary folk filed into the church behind them.

Jimmy's coffin looked small in front of the altar, draped with an American flag. The church was packed. The Zappalorti family sat in the front two rows. Cardinal O'Connor and Mayor Dinkins came to Mary and Michael and spoke with them. Mickey shook their hands. An altar boy came from behind the altar, made obeisance before the altar Crucifix and then led Cardinal O'Connor past the ranks of flower arrangements into the back of the church. At the chime of bells, the church became silent. The church organ sounded, and the choir began singing "Ave Maria." A procession of clergy and altar boys filed in from the front entrance and stopped at the center aisle of the church. When fully assembled, they processed down the center aisle to the rhythm of the music: four altar boys in white robes; the parish pastors, Monsignor Peter G. Finn and Monsignor John Gordon, walking in dignity side by side; Bishop Patrick V. Ahern following alone carrying a large gold cross; then Cardinal O'Connor; and finally two more altar boys bearing enormous candles.

The Holy Mass of Christian Burial began. Robert scanned the gathering until he finally found the faces of Detectives Larry Jensen and Bob Bergin in the church. They were seated in the rear. Monsignors Finn and Gordon have begun the solemn Mass. Twenty-five minutes into the rite, just before the administration of the Holy Communion, Cardinal O'Connor stood and walked to the pulpit. He adjusted the microphone, took in the entire congregation with his eyes, and began his eulogy.

"Today we put our differences aside and are joined here with the family and friends of James Patrick Zappalorti," Cardinal O'Connor began. "We pay our last respects to this gentle soul who was murdered last Monday, because he was gay."

Cardinal O'Connor lowered his gaze to the front pew. "Mrs. Zappalorti, you remarked to me before Mass that you think of Jimmy as a martyr to hatred. One of the reasons I'm here today is to forgive those who hate. But, at the same time, I remind everyone that the Roman Catholic Church unconditionally and categorically, condemns hatred and intolerance against anyone, including what was done to Jimmy. God loves each and every person no matter what their sexual orientation and calls for us to live in accordance with the teachings of the Church. We forgive those who murdered Jimmy. I remind you: The only answer to hatred is not more hatred; it is love. Love thy neighbor! I was told by his parents that Jimmy was a gentle person who loved working with stained glass with his family. He also loved playing the piano, gardening, and watching sunsets from the shack he'd built on the beach of the Arthur Kill River. I understand that these very windows in this church were made by Michael Zappalorti and his three sons," Cardinal O'Connor said.

"Look at their beauty as shafts of sunlight stream through these glorious stained glass windows. Jimmy and his family's artistic work surrounds us here today, as we pray for his soul."

The congregation sat in thoughtful silence at the Cardinal's words. The spiritual leader made the sign of the cross and bowed his head in prayer. Everyone else in the church followed, except for Robert, whose eyes were fixed on one of the stained glass windows.

"Jimmy and I had several things in common," Cardinal O'Connor continued. "We are both Catholics and love God. We were both in the United States Navy and served during the Vietnam War. Jimmy was a Seaman 1st Class, and I was an Admiral, Navy Chaplain and God's servant. Jimmy and I saw much horror during the Vietnam War, I'm sure those experiences caused Jimmy much pain and many feelings of isolation. I can certainly tell you that no one with sensitivity, with any humanity at all, could experience the evil that Jimmy saw and experienced without it searing into his innocent soul."

Cardinal O'Connor paused in prayer for a moment as soft organ music started to play the "Ava Maria" again. The Cardinal looked towards Mike and Mary Zappalorti in acknowledgment and then continued his eulogy. "However, because of his faith, I'm sure Jimmy has now passed through heaven's gate and has found everlasting peace."

"You're right, Cardinal! I know my Jimmy is in heaven!" Mary called out.

Because of her boldness, the rest of the surprised congregation turned to look at Mary.

"What did you say, Mary?" Cardinal O'Connor asked.

"I said, 'I know my Jimmy's in heaven.' I made a pact with God because I was worried that when me and my husband died, there would be no one to care for Jimmy. Well, through God's wisdom, He has taken care of my son. He's in heaven. Now I can carry my cross, my illness with peace of mind."

"You hear that folks? Mrs. Zappalorti just said "If God takes care

238

of her son, Jimmy, she would carry her cross. I am deeply moved by the Zappalorti family's tragedy and their abiding faith which has led you to bring forth a positive message from the loss of your son, a message of peace and love. I see no hatred here. I see extraordinary serenity and a deep, deep, belief that your son is in heaven.

"I'm now happy because my beloved son, Jimmy is happy," Mary said. "He is with God. God has answered my prayers. I don't have to worry about Jimmy anymore."

"What else can I say? On with the mass," Cardinal O'Connor proclaimed.

Hearing such a strong confession of faith from his Mother, Robert's felt himself buoyed up by the newfound faith. Robert stared in wonder at one of the stained glass windows. It depicted the Sacrifice of Isaac. In his mind's eye, suddenly Isaac's face became Jimmy's face. The face and eyes in the stained glass window turned and stared directly into Robert's eyes. It was the same smiling look Jimmy gave Robert the last time he saw him alive at the Beach House the summer before. Robert's grin stretched from ear to ear, as the organ music and the choir reached the climax of the sacred song.

The Mass was over, and the pallbearers had escorted the coffin down the aisle to the funeral hearse. The Zappalorti family and the rest of the attendees started leaving the church. The family waited outside near the entrance to thank people for coming to the service. Robert remained alone in the pew. His daughter Kelly came over to him, "Come Dad, let's join the rest of the family."

He and Kelly went outside and stood near Michael and Mary Zappalorti.

"Did you read Jimmy's letter last night, Bobby," Mary asked?

"Yes, Mom. I did," Robert said.

"Did it inspire you to write Jimmy's story and help answer your questions," Mary asked.

Robert smiled and nodded, yes. They turned and walked from the church to the waiting car.

Chapter 46 - Please Accept My Apology

THREE DAYS LATER, Mary was resting in her bedroom. She and Michael were still exhausted from the funeral and burial of their youngest son. Mike, Mickey, Peggy and Robert were seated around Mary's bed, talking. The phone rang. Peggy answered it.

"Hello, oh hi, Detective Jensen," Peggy said. "Tomorrow afternoon. Okay, I'll tell them. Thank you. Bye."

"What is it, Peggy?" Mary asked.

"The extradition is complete," Peggy informed. "Detectives Jensen and Bergin just wanted us to know that Philip Sarlo was back on Staten Island.

"That's good," Mary announced. "It brings me peace of mind and closure."

The doorbell rang. Peggy exited the room and walked to the front entrance. A minute later, she returned with an attractive but worried-looking, middle-aged woman. The woman looked as if she carried the weight of the world on her shoulders.

"Mom, Dad, this is Mrs. Patricia Taylor," Peggy said. "She's the mother of Michael Taylor. She asked to speak with you."

Looking somewhat embarrassed and nervous, Mrs. Taylor said, "I hope I'm not intruding, but I felt compelled to come see you in person."

Michael and Mary both said hello. Mary offered, "Please take your coat off and have a seat."

"No, I won't stay long," Mrs. Taylor said. After a pause she continued, "I just want to say how truly sorry I am for what my son Michael did to your son. Your son was always kind and helpful to me."

"Did you know, Jimmy?" Peggy marveled.

"Yes, he used to cut my lawn and trim my hedges. I paid him a little for his work. Jimmy always did a good job for me. I couldn't believe it when I learned my son had killed him. From the bottom of my heart, please accept my apology."

"Mrs. Taylor," Mary said. "I know how difficult this must be for you. It was not easy for you to come here, so we really appreciate the gesture. Thanks so much for coming." Mary thought for a moment while tapping her fingernails on the end table. "In a way, we've both lost our sons. My Jimmy is in heaven, and your son will be in jail for a long time."

Mrs. Taylor took her right hand and wiped a tear from her eye. She looked at Mary and Michael and said, "Your right, Mrs. Zappalorti, I have lost my son, too. I don't know how long he'll be gone – it could be for twenty-five years." Mrs. Taylor started to cry. "Please forgive me, but I must go now. Goodbye everyone. I'm sorry for your loss."

"Goodbye, Patricia, I'll keep you in my prayers," Mary said.

Peggy escorted Mrs. Taylor to the front door and watched her walk up the street. When she returned to the bedroom, she noted, "That was kind of her to come to the house and pay her personal respects."

"Yes, it was, Peggy," Mary said.

Mike made an unpleasant sound deep in his throat. He said, "At least she's remorseful for what her son did. Not like her lousy son."

Chapter 47 - Life Goes on by Planting Trees

ON THE NIGHT of January 24, 1990, Robert laid in bed without being able to sleep. When he looked at the glow of the electric clock, the digital numbers read 2:30 A.M. He was preoccupied with thoughts. He wanted to do something special for his late brother, something simple that Jimmy would have appreciated. Then he had the answer. Since Jimmy loved gardening and plants so much, he would plant three trees in his memory at the site he loved. The place where Jimmy spent the last day of his life on earth. The reason Robert chose to plant the trees by the river was because it was Jimmy's special place, the same place he decided to build his shack. There was a problem, however; the area at Jimmy's shack was all sand and gravel dredge spoil that contained little nutrients.

Hardwood trees would not thrive there. The solution was to plant evergreen trees, which did not require richly fertile soil. Robert lived in the heart of the Pine Barrens of southern New Jersey where millions of pitch pine and white pine trees grow. The climate and soils on the south shore of Staten Island were the same as the Pine Barrens. In fact, pitch pine and white pine trees were once native to Staten Island, although they are now rare in the wild. Thinking of planting the trees, Robert finally fell asleep.

A Memorial Day service was planned for Jimmy on May 28, 1990. The day before Robert went to an area of the Pine Barrens in

Ocean County, New Jersey dominated by pitch pine trees. He selected three healthy specimens that stood about 2.5 to 3 feet in height. He brought a spade and three five-gallon buckets to place the trees into (so the roots and soil would hold together during the trip to Staten Island). After carefully digging out the two pitch pine trees and one white pine tree from the sandy soil, he also collected some Sphagnum moss from a cedar swamp. The moss would be used to place around the roots to maintain moisture when the trees were planted. He watered the trees and placed them in the back of his Dodge Ram-charger.

The next morning Robert drove to Staten Island and arrived at his parent's house about 9:00 A.M. He borrowed his father's wheel barrel, so he could carry everything down in one trip. Pushing the wheel barrel in the soft gravelly sand was no easy task. The weight of the soil, trees and water made the trip difficult, as the rubber wheel bogged down in the soft sand. Robert stopped and rested a few times. The distance from the Zappalorti home to the selected planting area was less than a quarter of a mile.

From Androvette Street, the area where the shack was constructed was hidden by giant reeds and cattail in the wetland, and by black willow, red maple, gray birch, pin oak and sassafras trees on the sand bar. Jimmy had kept the road cut back and made a sturdy wooden bridge over the stream and muddy area, so that part of the trip was easy. The bridge had been damaged by the weight of the police vehicles and the ambulance that drove over it to reach the shack the day after Jimmy's murder.

After ten minutes of arduous wheeling, Robert arrived at the site where Jimmy was murdered. Some of the yellow crime scene tape was still in place. On the path, there were also patches of discolored sand from the dried blood.

The police detectives had completed their crime-scene investigation months before, so that the area was no longer off limits. Robert untied the yellow plastic tape and hung it on a tree, then took a shovel and walked to the dark, blood-stained spot in the sand. Using the bloody circle as the top corner, he marked out a perfect triangle. He made sure each point was ten feet distant from the adjacent points. While laying out the holes, he became very emotional. All the while he removed sand, he could feel Jimmy's presence. He stopped for a moment and said a prayer, asking God to bless his brother's soul and accept him into heaven.

Robert was amazed that Jimmy's blood had soaked down about two-inches into the sand. Once each hole was deep enough, he took the wheel barrel and filled it with leaves from the nearby gray birch, scarlet oak and sassafras trees. He lined the bottom of the hole with about four-inches of fallen leaves, which would become humus for the roots of the pine trees.

Then he took handfuls of Sphagnum moss and placed it equally around the top of the leaves forming a layer of about three inches. Robert took a pitch pine tree from the bucket and lowered it into each hole, making sure it was centered. Using his hands, he then took more moss and covered the roots with it, while mixing the sandy, blood-stained soil all around the roots. Using the shovel now, he took scoops of the sandy soil and packed it around the roots until the hole was completely back-filled. Keeping the pitch pine tree straight, he tamped the soil with the heel of his shoe, so it was well packed. When he had repeated the quasi-ritual two more times, he stepped back and admired the trees he had planted.

Each tree seemed to be reaching toward heaven. Robert watered the trees thoroughly, giving each one an equal amount until it was all gone. Robert's personal gesture for his younger brother was complete. The three trees would draw nourishment from the enriched sandy ground. For Robert, the three trees he had planted represented many things. One tree planted in the bloody soil was for Jimmy being reborn. His life's blood was now giving life to the tree. The other two trees in the triangle represented his mother and father, watching over Jimmy.

Another possible meaning, with a religious aspect was the three trees represented the Father, Son and Holy Ghost, since Robert's parents and brother, Jimmy were devout, church going Catholics. Aside from that, the trees would live there as a natural monument when Robert came to visit once in a while. When he looked at the trees, Robert would remember that this was Jimmy's special place on the river. It was his place where he dreamed of traveling the world and seeing places he'd read about in National Geographic magazines.

Jimmy was a frugal traveler and had the ability to stretch his money in order to visit all the places and countries he had marked on his destination wish list. In western United States, Jimmy had visited San Diego, Los Angeles, San Francisco, and the Grand Canyon. Another favorite destination was the Hawaiian Islands. In Europe, he visited Ireland (County Cork, where his grandmother and grandfather Ryan were born), Scotland, England, Paris, France, Florence, Genoa (the Italian city where Jimmy's grandfather Hector Zappalorti was born), Rome and Venice. However, each time he returned home to Staten Island, his shack on the river was still the place that made Jimmy the most happy and content. It was his sanctuary.

Chapter 48 - The Zappalorti Home: One Year Later

MICHAEL ENTERED MARY'S bedroom carrying a tray with coffee and a slice of apple pie. Mary was sitting in a chair next to her bed. Mickey, Peggy and Robert were seated around her. Mike set the tray down beside Mary, and also sat down.

"Well family," Mary said, "it's one year today since we lost our Jimmy."

"It's hard to believe it's been a year already," Mike said.

"I miss him around the studio and helping us install windows," Mickey said.

"Yeah, remember how he'd play the church piano or the organ instead of working," Mike recalled?

Everyone laughed and smiled at the memory. Suddenly the phone rang, interrupting the peaceful moment.

"I'll get it dad," Peggy said. "You rest."

Peggy walked to end table and picked up the phone.

"Hello, oh hi Detective Bergin," Peggy said. "What? Taylor and Sarlo's sentencing is finally happening? When is it? Oh, that soon. Yes, someone from the family will be there. Okay, I'll tell them. Thanks, good bye."

"What is it, Peggy," Mary asked?

"That was detectives Bergin," Peggy said. "He said that Taylor and Sarlo's sentencing is on January 3rd.

"Why, that's just two days away," Mary responded.

"Mickey and I have to set stained glass windows at a synagogue in Brooklyn that day, so we can't go," Mike said.

"I have to be in Pennsylvania for a bog turtle survey, so I can't go," Robert said.

"Unfortunately, I'm just too sick to go," Mary said.

"Well, since I'm not working, I guess it's up to me. I'll attend," Peggy announced.

On the morning of January 3, 1992, Peggy went to the Richmond County Supreme Court building. The courtroom was partially filled with people and several newspaper reporters. The District Attorney, William Murphy, was seated at the prosecutors table, and two public defenders, representing Taylor and Sarlo, were at the other table. Peggy walked to the front of the room and found a seat. The D.A. was reading a report. He looked up and smiled at her as Peggy sat. Detectives Jensen and Bergin entered the courtroom and sat in the front row, near Peggy. They said hello and waited for the court proceedings to start.

In a holding cell at the rear of the County Court House, Michael Taylor and Philip Sarlo sat waiting to go before the judge. They were dressed in orange jump suits with the words, Richmond County Jail written across the front and back. They were both in handcuffs and chain leg restraints. The phone rang and one of the officers answered it.

"Hello, oh they're almost ready for the prisoners. Okay we will get them ready," the court officer said.

The two officers fumbled with keys as they removed the handcuffs and leg restraints from Taylor and Sarlo. They escorted them through a corridor and waited by the door of the courtroom. The courtroom was filled with even more people now. Some were finding seats and others are whispering in conversation. The court clerk stood and said, "Everyone rise for his honor, Justice Norman J. Felig."

Everyone in the courtroom stood in silence as the judge entered the courtroom from his chambers. He sat down and looked at the assembled people.

"Please be seated," Judge Felig requested. "We're here this morning to sentence Michael Taylor and Philip Sarlo. Will the court guards bring in the two defendants?"

A door opened from the side of the courtroom. The two Court Officers escorted Michael Taylor and Philip Sarlo into the room. They slowly walked in front of the judge and stopped.

Their two lawyers, the Public Defenders, stood beside them. D.A. Murphy walked to the left side of them, and looked up at the judge.

"You have already read the court documents. Does the D.A. and the public defenders representing the defendants, Taylor and Sarlo, agree to the terms of the sentences I'm about to render," Judge Felig asked?

"Yes we do your Honor," both the two Public Defenders and D.A. Murphy replied simultaneously.

"Michael Taylor, for the crime of second degree murder, I hereby sentence you to 23-years to life." Judge Felig ordered. "For a subsequent burglary of the Zappalorti home, you are given a concurrent sentence of 5 to 15-years. You are hereby remanded to serve your time at the Clinton Correctional Facility, in Dannemora, New York. Do you have anything to say?"

"No," Michael Taylor coldly answered.

The judge was surprised at Taylor's attitude and uncaring manner. He made a notation on his file and turned his attention to Sarlo.

"Philip Sarlo, for the crime of second degree murder, I hereby sentence you to 18-years to life, Judge Felig remanded. "For a subsequent burglary of the Zappalorti home, you are given a concurrent sentence of 5 to 15-years. You are hereby remanded to serve your time at the Wende Correctional Facility, in Buffalo, New York. Do you have anything to say?"

"Yes your Honor," Sarlo replied. "I thought we were only going to rough Jimmy up. Teach him a lesson. That's what I agreed to. I never wanted to kill him. Taylor dragged me into this mess because he hated, Jimmy. Taylor's mother liked Jimmy because he used to cut her grass and trim her hedges, when Mike was in jail. Taylor was jealous of Jimmy, hated him, that's why he killed him. I'm sorry for what happened, your Honor. I apologize to the Zappalorti family. I'm truly sorry!"

"You fucking lying rat," Taylor yelled!

Outraged for revealing that personal information about him, Taylor came around the Court Officers. He angrily grabbed Sarlo by his throat, trying to strangle him. The Court Officers quickly subdued him and pulled him back. As they pulled Taylor back, he kicked Sarlo in the balls. Sarlo doubled over in pain. The Court Officers placed handcuffs on Taylor, with his hands behind his back.

"Mr. Taylor, this outburst will go on your permanent record," Judge Felig ordered. "Mr. Sarlo, I'll make a note that you were repentant. Remove the prisoners."

The next evening in the Zappalorti home, Mary sat in a chair with a blanket on her lap. Michael, Mickey, Peggy and Robert were seated around the room in conversation about what happened during the sentencing.

"Well Peggy, I'm touched that Sarlo was repentant and apologized to us for what he did to Jimmy," Mary said.

"I watched him, ma," Peggy replied. "He was very sincere. Taylor on the other hand, was not one bit remorseful. He said nothing."

"Michael Taylor is a scoundrel," Mary said. "He's the one who stabbed Jimmy."

"He had a mean look, ma," Peggy said. "He attacked Sarlo in the courtroom."

"I told you he had evil eyes," Mary said. "However, since Philip Sarlo, asked for our forgiveness, I'm going to write him a letter."

Two weeks later at the Wende Correctional Prison, in Buffalo, New York, Philip Sarlo was sitting in his prison cell reading a magazine. He looked older and the stress of prison life already showed on his face. A Prison Guard walked in front of his cell and stopped.

"Hey Sarlo," the guard said. "There's a letter for you. It's from the last person you would expect to hear from."

"Oh Yeah," Sarlo inquired. "Who's it from?"

"Read it and find out," the prison guard said.

The guard passed the letter through the bars to Sarlo. Sarlo took the letter and looked at the return address. His face revealed a surprised look. He sees it's from Jimmy's mother and is stunned that she would write him. He sat on his bunk and quickly opened the envelope. He starts to read the letter.

Dear Mr. Sarlo:

My daughter Peggy was at your sentencing. She told me that you expressed sorrow for your involvement in the murder of my son. When you were in my home the night you helped kill Jimmy, I could see fear in your eyes. Not anger or malice like Michael Taylor had in his eyes. Mr. Sarlo, I want you to know that many good things have happened because of Jimmy's murder. The Charleston Civic Association and the US Navy have dedicated plaques in my son's honor and planted a beautiful tree in front of my house. The gay and lesbian community and thousands of New York citizens have petitioned the politicians in Albany to pass a 'Hate Crimes Bill,' in Jimmy's name. Mayor Dinkins, Governor Cuomo, Senator Paterson and even Cardinal O'Connor have all contacted our family. Bert Coffman has founded the Zappalorti Society, in Jimmy's memory. So you see my son did not die in vain. He will be remembered long after I'm gone. That's why I forgive you, and that's why I will pray for you.

Sincerely, Mary T. Zappalorti.

Amazed that Jimmy's mother would forgive and pray for him was too much for Philip Sarlo to comprehend. He became overwhelmed with grief and sorrow. Within the bars of his prison cell, he dropped the letter onto his bed, placed his face into his cupped hands and began to cry passionately.

Chapter 49 - The Aftermath - and Beyond

THE FOLLOWING DAYS after Jimmy's murder, it was the lead story on all the major New York and New Jersey television news stations: CBS, NBC, ABC, and FOX News. Even the cable networks such as CNN highlighted the Zappalorti murder. Likewise, Jimmy's murder was headlined in all of the New York metropolitan area newspapers (including the New York Times), carried the developing story as it unfolded. The first television media reporters showed up on January 22, the same day that Mickey found Jimmy's body. They interviewed both Mike and Mickey, who gave brief statements to the press. Owen Reiter, the next door neighbor from across Androvette Street was also interviewed by television reporters and gave a statement about his friend, Jimmy.

As more was learned by the police investigation and the murderers arrested, Jimmy's story continued to merit airtime on all the network television news shows. The Zappalorti household was a busy place for weeks after the funeral. Phone calls from the news media and visits from family and friends continued. Mike and Mary received so many sympathy cards and letters of condolences from people all over the northeast United States that the dining room table was filled with them. Condolences were sent from the Congress of the United States, House of Representatives, from Governor Mario Cuomo, Staten Island Borough President Guy Molinari, and many other public officials. Hundreds of Mass cards and letters, from friends and strangers alike, brought comfort to the family.

The family also received a telegram from the Reverend Jesse

Jackson of the Rainbow Coalition. On the whole, the Zappalorti family felt that the media reported Jimmy's murder in a fair and balanced manner. The media acted respectfully and without too much sensationalism during the entire ordeal. The story of Jimmy's murder resonated on several different levels: as a hate crime in a period when crimes against homosexuals were getting more sympathetic media attention; in the Church, because the family was such staunch, yet tolerant, Catholics; the home burglary targeting holy articles; in the gay community, because one of their own had been so unjustly and inhumanely slain; and as a sensational murder in a quiet community on Staten Island.

Another important factor was Jimmy's murderers were quickly identified and captured because of the thorough and professional police work carried out by Detective Robert Bergin and Detective Larry Jensen. They took a personal interest in this case and worked diligently to find out who did it and why.

The two police detectives' thorough efforts did not go unnoticed by either the Zappalorti family or their superiors in the Police Department. In fact, Detectives Bergin and Jensen were both honored with an award in July, 1990 from the New York City Police Department and the Staten Island Advance newspaper as "Police Officers of the Month."

Because Jimmy's murder was classified as a hate crime, both Peggy Marlow and Robert Zappalorti were asked to be guests on the Geraldo Riviera Show on ABC television on September 19, 1991. Interest about Jimmy's murder continued in the New York area for several years afterwards, by politicians and political activists working toward getting the Hate Crimes Bill passed into law in the New York State Senate.

These events kept Jimmy's story and memory in the public eye during that time period. The term "hate crime" had first been used after a young black man was murdered by a mob of white teenagers in Howard Beach, New York, in December 1986. The term originally just included crimes motivated by prejudice against race, religion, or ancestry. In 1980, the Bias Incident Investigation Unit was begun in the New York Police Department, to compile statistics on crimes motivated by hatred of a particular class of people. In 1985, the list was expanded to include crimes based on sexual orientation. At the time of Jimmy Zappalorti's murder, no federal or New York state law protected homosexuals from hate crimes. A proposal to add the phrase "sexual orientation" to New York State's anti-bias crime law passed the State Assembly but was held up by the State Senate in 1988, because of those two words. The phrase "sexual orientation" was finally adopted and passed into law in the New York State Senate in 2000.

New York State now has an anti-bias crime law that protects homosexual women and men. There is only a limited national statute that prosecutes bias crimes which take place on federal property. Only thirteen states have state laws prosecuting hate crimes.

On Staten Island, the police investigation of Jimmy's murder was swift. Michael Taylor, age 20, was arrested in a bar in South Beach, Staten Island. He was taken into custody at the New Dorp 122nd Police Station and charged with second-degree murder. After police interviewed Taylor, they described him as "cold-blooded" and with "no remorse." He gave written and spoken statements freely and calmly admitting his involvement with the crime. Taylor told the police on videotape that he planned to kill Jimmy whether he had money or not, because as he was "just a gay." A source who knew Taylor described his attitude this way: "He never smiles...it's like he hates the world. He felt ugly, uneducated, and isolated from society." Taylor found a kindred spirit in Philip Sarlo, another high school dropout, one who also had a reputation as a troublemaker and heavy drinker. The two became friends around 1986, beginning a pattern of bouncing from job to job, mooching off friends and relatives, and committing petty crimes.

Michael Taylor's mother, Patricia, gave up her baby at birth because she was too young to care for him. He grew up with his grandparents in California. When Taylor was thirteen years old, he ran away for a few days and was apparently molested by a man. On his return, he was full of hatred against homosexuals and refused to speak about what had happened. Taylor's lawyer asked that his client be given a psychiatric evaluation to determine his mental fitness to stand trial, which the judge granted. No reason was found to delay Taylor's trial, for which he had initially pleaded "not guilty," but later changed his plea to guilty as part of a plea bargain.

Phillip Sarlo, 26, grew up on Joseph Avenue, on Staten Island. In 1990, he lived with his brother and another male friend. Sarlo did not harbor personal hatred against gays but was the type to go along with whatever his buddy, Taylor had started. The two street thugs started numerous fistfights at bars and strip clubs in the area. Sarlo's brother, Stephen, condemned him when notified of the murder of James Zappalorti. Stephen Sarlo said, "I think Phillip should rot in hell if he did that. I pity him. If he did this, he deserves what he gets." His father Wallace Sarlo said, "We hoped he would come out of prison better. But I guess he came out worse."

Sarlo escaped the net being drawn around him by making his way to the Port Authority in Manhattan and getting on a bus to Ocala, Florida. A confidential hot line was set up by detectives for information about his whereabouts. Detective Bergin circulated his description to police stations throughout the Metropolitan New York area. Sarlo was "a street urchin," Bergin said. "Where else is he going to go but the street?"

On February 2, 1990, Mayor David Dinkins made a personal condolence call on the Zappalorti family. He spent more than an hour in the home speaking with Mike, Mary and other family members. Robert Zappalorti videotaped the entire visit. When Mayor Dinkins entered Mary's bedroom, she was sitting-up in bed. She greeted the mayor cheerfully by saying, "hello Dave," as if he were an old friend. He held her hand and offered his sincerest sympathies to the entire Zappalorti family. It meant a great deal to the family that the Mayor of New York City would take time from his busy schedule. Mayor Dinkins further invited Peggy and Robert to come to his office for a press conference about Jimmy's murder the following week, which they both accepted.

On January 28, 1990, the entire Zappalorti family was gathered in Mary's bedroom once again. They were seated around Mary's bed, with the addition of their two longtime neighbors, Owen Reiter and Carol Kosa. Owen announced, "Mary, we have some good news for you and your family: The Charleston Civic Association has passed a resolution to have a memorial ceremony for Jimmy. The New York City Department of Parks is going to plant a tree for Jimmy. The Charleston Civic Association will provide an inscribed plaque dedicated to him." He paused for a moment and cleared his throat and then continued, "The plaque will read: 'This Tree Is in Memory of James Zappalorti. Our Town – His Town.'"

Matt Foreman and Bruce Kogan arrived with information about a New York State Crime Victims program that provided assistance. Foreman was an attorney with the New York City Gay and Lesbian Anti-Violence Project; Kogan came from the New York State Crime Victims Board. They carried paperwork for a claim. Families of crime victims are entitled in New York State to be compensated for the loss of property and/or the loss of a life. The money can be used to pay medical bills or the funeral of a murder victim. This claim was eventually approved.

Matt was clearly affected as he said, "Everything I read about you in the newspapers is a message of love and tolerance for gay people. The Coalition for Gay and Lesbian Rights will honor the family with a Certificate of Appreciation. I wish there were more families like yours."

It took months and, for some of the Zappalorti family, years to accept fully that Jimmy was gone. He would not be around to clean the streets of Charleston anymore; he could not play the piano in the living room nor help his mother keep the house clean. He was not around to work with his father and brothers in the stained glass business.

Don Shepler, missed Jimmy too, and he stayed in touch with Mary. When Jimmy's mother died in May, 1994, Don and his friend Lou attended Mary's funeral. Peggy and Bobby saw Don and Matt Forman one last time in the summer of 1995, when Peggy invited them for dinner at her home in New Jersey.

As promised, the Charleston Civic Association and the Knights of Columbus sponsored a dedication service for Jimmy on Memorial Day weekend in May1990. Cardinal John O'Connor attended, along with representatives of the U.S. Navy. The New York City Department of Parks' donated a red maple tree, and the Navy plaque for Jimmy's memory was installed.

On May 22, 1990, Mayor David Dinkins co-sponsored a New York City unity rally in conjunction with several Christian priests, ministers, and rabbis. The event was held at the Bethel United Methodist Church in Tottenville, Staten Island. Both Peggy Zappalorti-Marlow and Robert Zappalorti were asked to attend. Mayor Dinkins and several other politicians as well as clergy spoke at the rally. Bert Coffman was also asked to speak. Robert was asked to give a statement at the unity rally, which he did.

The following was the speech he gave at the memorial:

Bias and hate can come in many shapes and forms and from many verbal directions. It can be offensively obtrusive, when spoken in loud sharp words to the intended recipient. Hateful words may be uttered on a street corner, in an alley, in a bar, in a school or in a courtroom. On the other hand, prejudiced words may be whispered subtly, quietly in crafty, hushed tones. Such biased words can be spoken behind the backs of the recipients. Regardless of what form hateful words are spoken, the end result is the person or group they are directed at are caused much hardship and mental pain. Sometimes bias and hateful words will lead to cruel physical actions by a few individuals or by an out of control mob. My late brother, Jimmy Zappalorti was the target of such bias and hate on the night of January 22, 1990. Jimmy felt the hatred of Michael Taylor and Philip Sarlo through their verbal abuse and from the blade of Taylor's knife. They hated Jimmy simply because he was gay. Just because someone happens to be gay and is perceived as being 'different,' is that justification to hate them, harm them or take their life? I know that those here in this church are people of good will who have come together to help spread a message of tolerance, acceptance, and neighborly love in our communities, towns, and cities. We all share a common goal, which is through education and example, to spread the word of peace, understanding, and love of those who may be different from what is considered the 'norm.' If there is to be a gradual positive change in thinking, we all need to speak out whenever we hear or witness an injustice to a minority person. If we all do our part, we can make a difference. If each of us can just change the mind of one person and help him or her to be more tolerant of a minority, this will be a better city and place to live some day. We can all benefit from what our churches teach us, and that is, to 'Love thy neighbor.'"

Chapter 50 - Epilogue

THE FOLLOWING NOTE was published on September 23, 1990 in the bulletin of the St. Joseph - St. Thomas Parish, Staten Island, New York, by the Reverend Msgr. Peter G. Finn, Pastor:

Special Gift: Special thanks to Michael and Mary Zappalorti and their family and Michael and Sons Stained Glass Company for two beautiful stained glass windows of the Blessed Mother and the Divine Savior located inside the entrance of St. Joseph's Church. This beautiful donation is in memory of their son, James P. Zappalorti. He and they will always have a remembrance at our Masses and in our prayers.

Michael Taylor was initially sent to Kings County Medical Center, to undergo a psychiatric evaluation to determine whether he was capable of standing trial. The examination was requested at his arraignment by his defense attorney, who said Taylor was acting incoherently. The results of the examination revealed that he was psychologically stable to go before the scheduled hearing at Stapleton Criminal Court and mentally fit to be tried. Investigators described Taylor as cold-blooded. They say he sat and calmly answered questions about the brutal slaying of a gentle mentally disabled Vietnam veteran and showed no remorse. Taylor actively harassed the victim for months prior to the incident and told witnesses in advance that he intended to kill Jimmy Zappalorti because he was gay. He physically attacked and stabbed the victim to death. For this crime, Taylor was sentenced to 23 years to life. For a subsequent burglary of the Zappalorti home, he was given a concurrent sentence of 5 to 15-years. Taylor is currently serving his time in the Clinton Correctional Facility in Dannemora, New York. He will be eligible for parole in October, 2014.

Philip Sarlo knew James Zappalorti and apparently did not participate in the physical knife attack except as willing accomplice by holding the victim while Taylor did the stabbing. Sarlo was also a witness to the crime. He was sentenced to serve 18 years to life in prison. The maximum sentence for second degree murder in New York State is 25 years to life. The prosecuting attorney requested these slightly shorter sentences from the court, apparently in exchange for the defendants' willingness to plead guilty to second degree murder. The plea avoided the expense of a trial to the taxpayers of New York City and, more importantly, the stress that a trial would have placed upon the Zappalorti family.

While a fugitive in Florida, Sarlo exhausted his options and had nowhere else to run without money or friends. The Ocala police department nabbed him as he tried to escape. He was arrested on February 18, 1990 and held by the Ocala police. Sarlo appeared via closed circuit TV before Judge John Futch at the 5th Judicial Circuit Court in Ocala, Florida, from his holding cell in the Marion County Jail. Following a brief hearing, Judge Futch ordered Sarlo be held without bond and directed that a public defender be assigned to represent him. Barbara Gurrola, an assistant state attorney in Ocala, said, "Sarlo was charged with being a fugitive from New York on a homicide case and also charged with violating his parole. He'll be here until he waives extradition or decides to fight it. If Sarlo waives extradition, his return to New York could come within a matter of days." During interrogation, he admitted to assisting Taylor with Jimmy's murder. Sarlo also said he and Taylor were going to bury the body under an old row boat, but did not have shovels to complete the task, so they threw the body in the river.

Sarlo waived extradition and was taken back to Staten Island by two Ocala police detectives. Once in New York, he and Taylor faced trial for the murder of James Zappalorti. However, their defense attorney arranged a plea bargain with the prosecutor. While serving his prison sentence of 18 years to life at the Wende Correctional Institution, Philip Sarlo died. Although the details are lacking, ironically Sarlo died on May 30, 1997, at the age 33. Because he was not a family member, the author was unable to find out the exact cause of his death.

The New York State Hate Crimes Bill. After years of contemplation and debating, an agreement was finally reached by politicians in Albany, New York. On July 10, 2000, New York State Governor George Pataki signed into law a hate crimes bill that passed both houses of the Legislature on June 23, 2000. The measure, which enhances penalties for hate motivated offenses, including crimes motivated by anti-gay hate, is the first statewide law in the history of New York State to specifically include protection for lesbian women and gay men.

Matt Foreman said after the bill was signed: "It would be disingenuous not to acknowledge the fact that two words in the legislation, 'sexual orientation,' kept us from this day for ten years. While we struggled over the last decade to reach this day, thousands of New Yorkers, including over 6,000 lesbian and gay people in New York City alone, became victims of hate violence. All of those people in general, and Jimmy Zappalorti in particular, are with us here today in spirit as we sign into law this hate crimes bill." Matt Foreman was the Executive Director of the National Gay and Lesbian Task Force between May 2003 and May 2008. The National Gay and Lesbian Task Force Foundation was founded in 1973 and is the first national lesbian, gay, bisexual and transgender (LGBT) civil rights and advocacy organization. This dedicated group remains the LGBT movement's leading voice for freedom, justice and equality. The Task Force works to build the grassroots political strength in the community by training state and local activists and leaders, working to strengthen the infrastructure of state and local allies, and organizing broad-based campaigns to build public support for complete equality for LGBT people. Their Policy Institute, the community's premier think tank, provides research and policy analysis to support the struggle for complete equality. As part of a broader social justice movement, the agency works to create a world that respects and makes visible the diversity of human expression and identity where all people may fully participate in society. The organization is headquartered in Washington, D.C.; however, they also have offices in New York City, Los Angeles, Cambridge, Massachusetts and Miami, Florida. The Task Force is a 501(c)(3) corporation incorporated in Washington, D.C. Contributions to the Task Force are tax deductible to the full extent allowed by law. Matt Foreman has heroically worked for more than 25 years to secure human rights for LGBT people.

Don Shepler, Jimmy's best friend and long-time companion stayed in touch with Mary Zappalorti until she died in 1994. Don remained at his apartment in Greenwich Village until 1999. Don was dancing at a friend's birthday party in Greenwich Village, New York City when he collapsed due to a heart attack and died. He was 54 years old.

Robert "Bert" Coffman, who was so inspired by Jimmy's tragic story, founded the Zappalorti Society. This is a nonprofit, active support group for lesbian, gay, bisexual, or transgendered people who suffer from stress and mental illness. On January 15, 2007, Bert Coffman wrote the following letter from the Zappalorti Society:

Dear Bob,

We remember your brother Jimmy's dates. This year January 23rd falls on a Tuesday when we have our Cheese and Bread group at the "Rainbow Heights Club," in Brooklyn. We remember Jimmy, so he has not died in vain. We advocate for all the people like him and the millions of gay people who suffer from mental health problems in America who cry out for help like Jimmy. So many of these people need assistance with their mental health problems from groups like ours and from city and state social services.

At the time of this writing, the Zappalorti Society still meets on 13th Street and Seventh Avenue in New York City every Saturday from 2:00 to 4:00 P.M. Those who wish to contact the Zappalorti Society may do so at (917) 286-0616.

One of Bert's friends, Russell Skop, who attends these meetings on occasion, authored this report about The Zappalorti Society: Many issues ago I wrote of my autobiography and my manic-depressive illness. I want to share with you some information, history, thoughts and feelings on a great lesbian, gay, bi-sexual, and transgender rap-support group that I attend. It is called The Zappalorti Society and meets every Saturday from 2 P.M. to 4 P.M. at the Lesbian, Gay, Bi and Transgender Community Center located on 13th Street and Seventh Ave in New York City. The Zappalorti Society is described in the Community Center's newsletter as a group for psychiatric survivors organized for peer support, self-help and mental health advocacy. Would you like to know why we are called The Zappalorti Society? Jimmy Zappalorti was a Vietnam Naval Veteran. He was gay. Sometimes gay guys do go into the military. He served in the Navy, but became mentally ill and was discharged from the Navy. He lived on Staten Island with his parents. The short version of a long story is that Jimmy Zappalorti was gay and mentally ill, did odd jobs around his home, played with neighborhood kids and he even built himself a shack near his parent's home on the Arthur

Kill River waterway. Before Jimmy was killed, he was harassed several times by Michael Taylor and Philip Sarlo, but Jimmy did not tell anyone because he was mentally handicapped and the incidents went unnoticed. Then in January 1990, Jimmy Zappalorti was killed by the same thugs from a nearby bar. Jimmy Zappalorti's death brought the Dinkins Mayoral Administration to action and the killing of course was a gay-bashing. Mr. Coffman, the leader of our current group teaches all the members of The Zappalorti Society the history of Jimmy Zappalorti and we remember the anniversary of the sad slaying. Feel free to come any Saturday to learn more! On the lighter side the group is always one of the best attended, sometimes gets noisy and laughing goes on any given Saturday afternoon. But we are serious when someone has an issue, problem or crisis. We are there for each other not just for fun & games. Bert Coffman (917-286-0616) is our leader and permits an open forum. Of course, like any group, if too much cross-talk goes on, Mr. Coffman carefully structures the discussions. Our talks include but are never limited to: how we take our medicine or what we take; our diagnosis if we choose to share that; our relationship problems; fun things and social stuff including: movies, theater, TV, etc. Besides our group leader and of course everybody in the group helping each other there is a psychiatrist who attends our group at least once a month or so to see how the group is doing. Her name is Dr. Melanie Spritz, D.O. She is excellent with the group and everyone looks forward to seeing her when she comes. Dr. Melanie is what she likes to be called, and can be found on the American Medical Association web page on the internet for further information. In conclusion and on a brighter note the Rap-Support Group I've described above I consider my weekly dose of needed fresh air. I love the group. All you have to do is basically take almost any train or bus to 14th Street near 7th Avenue and walk over to the Center at 208 West 13th Street, New York City 10011. The telephone number is: 212-620-7310. We (the group) go for a meal afterwards too. Try it, you'll like it *(written by Russell Skop, 2007)*."

James Smith, a former New York Corrections Officer (retired), and now a reporter for the Staten Island Advance (and blogger on their web site), has also been helpful to the Zappalorti family. On September 10, 2012, Jim wrote an article in the Staten Island Advance (and on their web site), titled: "A Plea to Keep a Killer in Prison," because Michael Taylor became eligible for parole on October 2012. Dozens of friends and family wrote to the New York State Parole Board, requesting that Taylor's parole be denied. Thanks to all who wrote letters, especially Jim Smith and the Richmond County District Attorney's Office, Taylor's parole was denied. However, he will become eligible for release consideration again in October 2014.

Mary T. Zappalorti was a loving wife and dedicated mother. Mary and Michael were married on February 4th, 1934 in Brooklyn, New York and had four children together. She loved her family and devoted her life to them. She was a devout Catholic and made sure her four children went to Catholic grammar school. Mary loved to do crossword puzzles. She wrote her own crossword puzzle dictionary which took her five years on an old Remington typewriter. She tried to get it published, but someone else had just published a similar book six months earlier with the same idea. To her dismay, it was never published. On May 4, 1994, Mary died in her sleep of complications from the emphysema she had suffered from. She and Mike were married for sixty-years. She was 78-years old when she passed away. Mary was buried on Staten Island with her husband of 61-years, Michael, her two sisters, Nora and Regina Ryan, along with her son, James Zappalorti.

Michael A. Zappalorti Sr., as he grew older, went to mass every day. At age 77, he was semi-retired and no longer worked daily at his craft of stained glass. However, Michael still supervised repair work and the new windows that his son made and installed in churches all around Staten Island and New York. He and his son, Michael Jr., considered themselves artists as well as tradesmen. Their work place, Michael & Sons Stained & Leaded Glass Studios, was located next to the family home in the South Shore, Charleston community where the senior Zappalorti has called home since 1950. Michael Zappalorti began in the Stained Glass business as a young man. His father, a native of Genoa, Italy, like his father before him, taught Zappalorti and his brothers the fine art of the stained glass trade. The young men brought their knowledge and skills to the States, and today, a generation later, Zappalorti and his son have an impressive list of some 30 churches on Staten Island, and scores of others in the metropolitan area, on the West Coast and in Canada, in which their artistic glass work appears. Additionally, a number of restaurants and residences boast the Zappalorti stained glass touch, too. Michael Zappalorti, Sr. said, "Stained glass is something that lasts for a lifetime. Sometimes I go back to a church where my windows were installed and sit in a pew and look at the windows. It is like an old book; it doesn't fade away." Due to complications from prostate cancer, Michael Zappalorti Sr. died on September 5, 1994, four months after his beloved wife, Mary died. He had kept his illness at bay through sheer determination, while nursing Mary in her last days. Once she died, he lost his will to fight, and the cancer spread throughout his body. He was 81 years old. Mike was buried alongside Mary and Jimmy on Staten Island.

James P. Zappalorti...as a child and young teenager, Jimmy frequently helped his parents. He loved working in the Stained Glass Studio and was affectionately called, "Dad's little helper." Jimmy always wanted to be a glazier like his father. He also admired his oldest brother Mickey, and wanted to be a sailor in the Navy, just like his brother and his uncle Martin Ryan were. James Zappalorti, whose killing was the first crime in New York City history to be officially identified by the New York City Police Department as a murder inspired by bias because the victim was gay. The crime shocked the small, isolated community of Charleston, near the southern end of Staten Island, where both Taylor and Zappalorti lived. Jimmy lived on a disability pension with his elderly parents. He was well known and liked by most of his neighbors. Jimmy's so-called, "beach house" and dock are now in ruins; but the three pine trees his brother, Bobby, planted in the summer of 1990, right at the place where Jimmy died, are alive and growing. The memorial pine trees are now over 25-feet tall. Jimmy's memorial in front of the Zappalorti Glass Studio is still there. The plaques in honor of Jimmy from the Charleston Civic Association and from the US Navy are positioned on either side of the red maple tree. Jimmy is buried at the same plot with his mother and father on Staten Island, New York.

Sister Mary Athanasius, who taught Jimmy in the 7th and 8th grades at Our Lady Help of Christians School, in Tottenville said: "He was a wonderful boy. I know he's in heaven now. We can pray to him now, and not for him, because Jimmy is a member of the communion of saints." James Patrick Zappalorti was 44 years old at the time of his murder.

Michael A. "Mickey" Zappalorti Jr. is now retired. Mickey sold the family stained glass business that was located in Charleston in the summer of 2009. Now that he has the time, Mike loves to ride his Harley Davidson motorcycle with his friends. He was in poor health for a while after battling cancer, but has beaten the dreaded disease for now. Mike, like his father, spends his spare time collecting stamps. Sadly, the Zappalorti glass business has come to an end, because none of the Zappalorti grandchildren had the desire or passion to work in the stained glass business.

Peggy Zappalorti-Marlow is a retired legal and real estate secretary. She now lives in Woodbridge, New Jersey with her second husband, Richie Marlow. Two of Peggy's children, Ronald and Barbara live in Claremont, California, while her other two daughters live in Woodbridge, New Jersey. Peggy has become an advocate for lesbian, gay, bisexual and transgender civil rights. She has been on numerous radio and television programs to promote public awareness, not only for the memory of Jimmy but also for all lesbian and gay issues.

Robert T. Zappalorti continues to run his environmental consulting business, Herpetological Associates, Inc., Plant and Wildlife Consultants, with offices in New Jersey and Pennsylvania. He is also an accomplished photographer, writer and actor. Working in his spare time, he wrote three different drafts of this book over a span of fifteen years. On November 30, 2007, Robert partnered with Edward EmanuEl, a Professor of Theater Arts, at California State University, Fresno. Together, they wrote a companion screenplay for a movie about the Zappalorti family saga and his late younger brother, James P. Zappalorti, entitled "Stained Glass Windows."

Memories of a Life Cut Short

Michael Sr. and Jimmy making a window in the studio

272

*Mary and Jimmy outside
the glass studio*

Jimmy Zappalorti - 1963 Navy Photo

USS Henrico
and
Jimmy's Navy Plaque

JAMES P. ZAPPALORTI
SN   US NAVY
VIETNAM
SEP 29 1945   ✝   JAN 23 1990

Police at Jimmy's beach house

*Michael
Taylor*

*Philip
Sarlo*

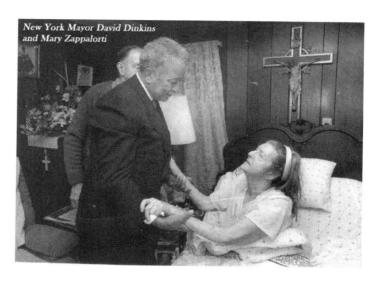

New York Mayor David Dinkins
and Mary Zappalorti

Mike Zappalorti Sr.
in the family living room
in 1990

THIS TREE IS IN MEMORY OF
JAMES ZAPPALORTI
1943 — 1990
OUR TOWN — HIS TOWN
CHARLESTON CIVIC ASSOCIATION

Kelly and Bobby Zappalorti at Jimmy's Memorial

278

Bibliography

BRISAR, CATHERINE. *A Thousand Years of Stained Glass.* Arnoldo Mondedori, Editor. Milan, Italy: S. P. A. Publishers, 1986.

Brownstone, David, Irene M. Franck, and Douglass Brownstone. *Island of Hope, Island of Tears.* New York: Barnes and Noble, Inc., 2000.

Burns, Rick and James Sanders with Lisa Ades. *New York: An Illustrated History. The Companion Volume to the Television Series.* New York: Alfred A. Knopf, 1999.

Carlo, Philip. *The Ice Man, Confessions of a Mafia Contract Killer.* Saint Martin's Griffin Press, New York, New York. 2006.

Chin, Yvette, editor. *Faith • Hope• Light: The Art of the Stained Glass Windows.* Philadelphia: Courage Books, a division of Running Press, 1999.

Clendinen, Dudley and Adam Nagourney. *Out For Good: The Struggle to Build a Gay Rights Movement.* New York: Simon & Schuster, 1999.

Cothran, Helen, book editor. *Homosexuality: Current Controversies.* Farmington Hills, Michigan: Greenhaven Press, 2003.

Davis, Kenneth C. *Don't Know Much About The Bible: Everything You Need To Know About The Good Book But Never Learned.* New York: Eagle Brook, William Morrow and Company, Inc., 1998.

Eron, John Lewis. "Homosexuality and Judaism." in *Homosexuality and World Religions.* Arlene Swidler, editor. Valley Forge, Pennsylvania:

Trinity Press International, 1993.

Eskridge, William N. Jr. Gaylaw: *Challenging the Apartheid of the Closet*. Cambridge Massachusetts: Harvard University Press, 1999.

Fone, Byrne. *Homophobia: A History*. New York: Metropolitan Books, Henry Holt and Company, 2000.

Gomes, Peter J. *The Good Book: Reading The Bible With Mind and Heart*. New York: William Morrow and Company, 1996.

Heide, Robert and John Gilman. *Greenwich Village: A Primo Guide to Shopping, Eating, and Making Money in True Bohemia*. New York: St. Martin's Griffin, 1995.

Highsmith, Carol and Ted Landphair. *New York City: The Five Boroughs, a Photographic Tour*. New York: Random House Inc., 1997.

Holy Bible: New Analytical Indexed Bible. Chicago: John A. Dickson Publishing Company, 1931.

Ishay, Micheline R. *The History of Human Rights: From Ancient Times to the Globalization Era*. Los Angeles: University of California Press, 2004.

The Jerusalem Bible. Alexander Jones, General Editor. London: Darton, Longman & Todd, 1968.

Kaufman, Gershen and Lev Raphael. *Coming Out Of Shame: Transforming Gay and Lesbian Lives*. New York: Main Street Books, Doubleday, 1996.

Kugle, Scott and Siraj al-Haqq. "Sexuality, diversity, and ethics in the agenda of progressive Muslims." in *Progressive Muslims*. Omid Safi, editor. Oxford: Oneworld, 2003.

Lee, Lawrence, George Seddon, and Francis Stephens. Stained Glass. New York: Crown Publishers Inc., 1976.

Lopate, Phillip. Waterfront: *A Journey Around Manhattan*. New York: Crown Publishers Inc., 2004.

MacMullen, Ramsay. *Christianizing the Roman Empire (A.D. 100-400)*. New Haven, Connecticut: Yale University Press, 1984.

Marshall, Jo. Glass Sourcebook: *A Visual Record of the World's Great Glass Making Traditions*. Secaucus, New Jersey: Chartwell Books,

Inc., 1990.

McGarry, Molly and Fred Wasserman. *Becoming Visible: An Illustrated History of Lesbian and Gay Life in Twentieth-Century America.* New York: The New York Public Library, Penguin Studio, 1998.

Merriam-Webster's Encyclopedia of World Religions. Wendy Deniger, Consulting Editor. Springfield, Massachusetts: Merriam-Webster Inc., 1999.

Miller, Neil. *Out of the Past: Gay and Lesbian History from 1869 to the Present.* New York: Vintage Books, 1995.

Mollenkott, Virginia Ramey. *Sensuous Spirituality: Out From Fundamentalism.* New York: Crossroad Publishing Company, 1993.

Oliver, Marilyn Tower. *Gay and Lesbian Rights: A Struggle.* Springfield, New Jersey: Enslow Publishing Inc., 1998.

Panati, Charles. *Sacred Origins of Profound Things: The Stories Behind the Rites and Rituals of the World's Religions.* New York: Penguin Books USA Inc., 1996.

Scanzoni, Letha Dawson and Virginia Ramey Mollenkott. *Is the Homosexual My Neighbor? A Positive Christian Response.* HarperSanFrancisco, Harper Collins, Inc., 1994.

Scull, Theodore W. *The Staten Island Ferry.* New York: Quadrant Press Inc., 1982.

Shilts, Randy. *And the Band Played On: Politics, People, and the AIDS Epidemic.* New York: St. Martin's Press, 1987.

Smith, Dr. William. *Smith's Bible Dictionary, Revised Edition.* Philadelphia: A.J. Holman Corp.(no publishing date).

Stane, Stephen P., Roger G. Panette and Brian E. Forist. *The Hudson: An Illustrated Guide to the Living River.* New Brunswick, New Jersey: Rutgers University Press, 1996.

Streissguth, Tom. *Hate Crimes.* New York: Library In A Book, Facts on File, Inc., 2003.

Walke, Nancy. *All About Stained Glass.* Blue Ridge Summit, Pennsylvania: Tab Books, 1982.

Wetzsteon, Ross. *Republic of Dreams: Greenwich Village, The*

American Bohemia, 1910-1960. New York: Simon & Schuster, 2002.

Whitaker, Brian. *Unspeakable Love: Gay and Lesbian Life in the Middle East*. Los Angeles, University of California Press, 2006.

Zindel, Paul. *The Pigman and Me*. New York: A Charlotte Zolotow Book, Harper Collins, 1991.

Made in the USA
Charleston, SC
22 September 2014